WRITERS AND THEIR WORK

ISOBEL ARMSTRONG
General Editor

BRYAN LOUGHREY
Advisory Editor

LEO TOLSTOY

Hulton Deutsch Collection

LEO TOLSTOY

LEO TOLSTOY

John Bayley

NORTHCOTE

BRITISH COUNCIL

ATLANTIC
PUBLISHERS & DISTRIBUTORS (P) LTD

This edition is published by
ATLANTIC
PUBLISHERS & DISTRIBUTORS (P) LTD
7/22, Ansari Road, Darya Ganj, New Delhi-110 002
Tel: 40775252, 23273880, 23275880, 23280451; Fax: +91-11-23285873
E-mail: orders@atlanticbooks.com; Web: www.atlanticbooks.com

By arrangement with
Northcote House Publishers Ltd
Horndon House, Horndon, Tavistock, Devon, PL19 9NQ,
United Kingdom. (T)+44(0)1822 810066; (F)+44(0)1822 810034
(E) northcote.house@virgin.net and (W) www.northcotehouse.co.uk
The *Writers and their Work* series is published in association with the British Council.

First Indian Reprint 2010
First published in 1997 by Northcote House Publishers Ltd

ISBN 978-81-269-1308-4

British Library Cataloguing-in-Publication Data
A catalogue record for this book is available from the British Library

Typeset by PDQ Typesetting, Newcastle-under-Lyme
Printed in India at Nice Printing Press, A-33/3A, Site-IV,
Industrial Area, Sahibabad, Ghaziabad, U.P.

Contents

Acknowledgements

In writing this study, I am most grateful to Professor Neil Cornwell of Bristol University for his meticulous contribution in compiling the valuable biographical outline and up-to-date bibliography.

Preface

Much of the writing even of such a great and world-famous figure as Tolstoy comes in the end to seem dead wood. His theories and polemics once impressed and influenced thousands, indeed millions, of readers, and sometimes changed their lives: but with time these writings necessarily have given up much of the life and force that was once in them. New generations have turned to new ideologies, and tried to find fresh spiritual solutions to life's problems.

But Tolstoy's art – the art that he himself came to reject or despise when he settled into the grip of his own later convictions – does not change; it remains as lively, as fascinating and as absorbing as ever. *War and Peace* and *Anna Karenina* will continue to delight their readers, and draw them irresistibly into a uniquely spacious and complex world, as long as there are any readers left at all. And these works will continue as well to exercise a profound influence on the best imaginative writing. In our own time Vikram Seth's novel *A Suitable Boy*, as long as *War and Peace* and clearly inspired by it, has become – and deservedly – a world best-seller.

It is for this reason that I have concentrated in this short introduction to Tolstoy on his two greatest novels, and the ancillary texts and tales that relate to them. I make no apology for passing more rapidly over Tolstoy the prophet, preacher and reformer, because these sides of his work, while far from having become mere curiosities, can no longer speak to us with the power and originality of those masterpieces which we shall always continue to discover, discuss and explore.

What would Tolstoy feel about the ideological movements of our time, racial and ecological issues, feminism, political correctness? With much of what we now take for granted here he himself would probably have agreed; and yet there are few great writers who demonstrate such single-minded independence as Tolstoy did. Wholly 'inner-directed', as we should say today, he spent the first part of his life as a writer and thinker examining and analysing with a ruthless and penetrating intelligence every system and fashion of thought which his century produced in such abundance, and rejecting them all. Kant, Hegel, Schopenhauer, Rousseau – none of them would do, although at one time or another all of them attracted his admiration and his intensive study.

His independence was essentially that of an aristocrat and conservative, a man without vanity, but with complete confidence in his own mental processes. He despised then, and would despise now, a society's need to conform; and the intellectual's need to be on the side of conventional enlightenment, and whatever may be the current radical programme. He was not in the least afraid of appearing reactionary to his intellectual acquaintances; but at the same time – for example on the position of women – his views could be more radical than theirs, as well as more sensible. He disliked and distrusted all cults and movements, and soon wished nothing more than to escape from the one he had involuntarily created. Fanaticism, even in its kindest and most harmless forms, bored or repelled him; and nothing came to irritate him so much in his last years as a Tolstoyan. But he often loved and respected them individually: it was human individuality to which up to the end he was most strongly attracted, and which he most profoundly understood.

Biographical Outline

1812	Napoleon invades Russia.
1815	Battle of Waterloo.
1825	(14 December) Decembrist uprising in St Petersburg. Accession of Nicholas I.
1828	(28 August) Lev Tolstoy born at Yasnaya Polyana.
1830	Death of Tolstoy's mother.
1837	Death of Pushkin. Family moves to Moscow. Death of Tolstoy's father.
1841	Death of Lermontov.
1844–7	Studies at Kazan university.
1847	Leaves university without a degree. Inherits Yasnaya Polyana.
1848–9	Year of European revolutions.
1851	Enlists as army volunteer in the Caucasus.
1852	Death of Gogol. *Childhood* published.
1854	*Boyhood*.
1854–5	Commissioned and serves in Crimea: writes *The Sebastopol Sketches*. Crimean War (1854–6).
1855	Death of Nicholas I. Return of surviving Decembrist exiles.
1856–7	Flaubert publishes *Madame Bovary*.
1857	*Youth* (third part of trilogy). Travels in Europe.
1859	*Family Happiness* ('Happy Ever After'). Goncharov publishes *Oblomov*.
1860–1	Further European travels.
1861	Liberation of the serfs.
1862	Marries Sofya Andreyevna Behrs.
1863	*The Cossacks*. Birth of first child. Turgenev publishes *Fathers and Sons*.

1863–9	Works on and publishes *War and Peace*. Three more children.
1866	Dostoevsky publishes *Crime and Punishment*.
1870	Death of Dickens.
1870–1	Franco-Prussian War. Paris Commune.
1871–2	George Eliot publishes *Middlemarch*.
1873–7	Works on *Anna Karenina*.
1878	Spiritual crisis and so-called 'conversion'.
1879–81	*A Confession*.
1880	Dostoevsky publishes *The Brothers Karamazov*.
1881	Death of Dostoevsky. Assassination of Alexander II.
1883	Death of Turgenev.
1886	*The Death of Ivan Ilyich* and play, *The Power of Darkness*.
1888	Birth of thirteenth and last child.
1889	*The Kreutzer Sonata* (banned in 1890). Begins *Resurrection*.
1893	Major theological work, *The Kingdom of God is Within You*.
1894	Accession of Nicholas II.
1894–5	*Master and Man*.
1897	*What is Art?* (treatise on aesthetics).
1898	Organizes aid for Dukhobors.
1899	Completes *Resurrection*.
1901	Excommunicated from Orthodox church.
1904	Death of Chekhov. Completes *Hadji Murad* (published posthumously).
1905	'First' Russian revolution.
1908	*I Cannot Be Silent!* (treatise against capital punishment).
1909	Correspondence with Gandhi.
1910	Runs away from home. (7 November) falls ill and dies at Astapovo railway station.

1

Life and Background

Leo Tolstoy was born in 1828 at Yasnaya Polyana in the province of Tula, 120 miles south of Moscow. He had three elder brothers — Nikolai, Sergei and Dmitri – and after giving birth to a daughter Maria, always known as Masha, his mother died when he was only 2 years old. Such a bereavement was so common in those days that it was taken for granted, by the deprived child and by the rest of the family, and it is only with the psychological hindsight of today that the possible consequences have become of theoretical interest. Loss of a mother, and Tolstoy always claimed afterwards that he had been especially close to his, can have a permanent effect on adult mentality and outlook. Tolstoy came near to claiming, in his last years, that he had never really grown up. He remembered, he said, the slippery sides of the wooden bowl in which is mother had bathed him, and such memories came to him all the more vividly at the time of his own death. 'As I was then, so am I now', he said when he was an old man of 82.

Certainly he had an uncanny gift for remembering and describing childhood and childhood sensations: more than that, the descriptions and the tone of reality in all his great stories and novels possess the air of something seen and apprehended for the first time, as a child might see it. The formalist critic Shklovsky, one of his most brilliant and detailed commentators, has pointed out that not only are things seen in Tolstoy's writing as if never before, but they have for this reason a permanent air of the surprising and the unfamiliar. Tolstoy's descriptions, said Shklovsky, 'make it strange'. That is to say we are present as readers at a party, or at a battle or a ballet, as a child might be present, seeing everything not in its conventional familiar shapes as an adult sees it, but as a primary phenomenon – strange or wonderful or terrifying. Tolstoy's novels abound in illustrations of this, and sometimes in his didactic way he makes a special point of it. When Natasha in *War and Peace* goes to the ballet for the first time she cannot see the point of a man in comic tights waving his legs about; it all seems to her affected and ridiculous. But from other people's reactions, and from what she hears and is told, she soon comes to accept the normal evaluation and appreciation of the art. In this context she has learnt quickly to be no longer natural or child-like.

Tolstoy taught children on his country estate all his life, and observed their reactions closely. Significantly perhaps, he was more fond of children met in that sort of way than he was of his own family, at least of his sons. For although that deprivation in early life proved a marvellous asset to his writing genius, it left him in many ways not well fitted for family life. 'The family is hell' he once remarked succinctly, and the paradox of his life and reputation is that he became a seer and a patriarch while at the same time secretly and violently rejecting all the consequences of what must always and ultimately have been for him a false position, and one which made him in his own eyes a false prophet.

His marriage for a start. In his stories and novels he shows himself to be an expert on marriage, and all the marriages he describes so well are based on his own, not even excluding the loveless marriage of Anna and her husband in *Anna Karenina*, and her long and finally fatal liaison with Vronsky. Tolstoy knew it all from the inside. For writers in the midst of the nineteenth century marriage was virtually an unexplored territory, and it was Tolstoy's greatest strength as a writer to be an inflexibly curious explorer of what such things in human life were really like, as a child may reveal that the emperor has no clothes. No detail was too trivial for him to miss, no arrangement too ordinary to escape his sharpest scrutiny. 'Truth is my hero', he once proclaimed; and although, as we shall see later on, this claim can in itself not be quite true, he is always as disconcertingly perceptive in matters of fact as that tiresome child who sees that the emperor has nothing on. This unerring sense of things commonly ignored in life, and of the minor but decisive moments in living, makes, in the end, the supreme pleasure of reading and re-reading him.

His family on both sides belonged to the old Russian aristocracy. His mother, Princess Maria Nikolayevna, was a

Volkonsky; and the Tolstoys themselves were a large tribe who had produced many well-known and colourful and indeed notorious figures in Russian history. A distant cousin was known as Tolstoy the American, not because he had settled in the United States but by reason of his being a famous eccentric, duellist and explorer, a man who, like Dolokhov in *War and Peace,* who got drunk and wrestled with bears. Other members of the family had been important and often crooked diplomats for the tsars, including the Tolstoy who had lured the Tsarevich Alexei back to Russia from Turkey, and into the clutches of his terrible father, Peter the Great. Tolstoy was not only proud of his name and forebears but he took his status in Russian life absolutely for granted. Even when in his later days he sought to behave like a peasant, and to live simply and humbly, he always remained underneath the *barin,* the master who knows he will be respected and obeyed. As many of his critics have pointed out, Tolstoyan humility is always as ambiguous as Tolstoyan faith and belief.

On his mother's side the Volkonskys had also been distinguished, mostly as generals and army commanders, and there was something military about Princess Maria herself. She seems to have been rather a silent and severe woman, very devout in her religious observances, and always obeying but not getting on too well with her indolent and worldly husband, whose idea of a good life was hunting and lounging about the estate. In her own reserved and distant way she seems to have been kind to her youngest son; and perhaps it was her very shyness and lack of intimacy which caused him to romanticize her later on, as the source of all that was good and vanished in his life, while at the same time valuing and celebrating feminine warmth and affection, of the kind that he was to obtain after his mother's death from his aunt Tatiana, a model for Sonya in *War and Peace.*

But life for the young people at Yasnaya Polyana was always sufficiently idyllic. Tolstoy describes it superbly in *Childhood,* which is unique among books of its kind in focusing on the psychology of a group of children as it changes and develops from day to day. The author seems simultaneously to *be* a child and to be analysing and understanding what it is *like* to be one. It is rather droll, too, to contrast the narrator of *Childhood* with the little boy whom his family afterwards remembered and wrote their recollections of, particularly his sister Masha. She was of course younger, the youngest of the family, and, though she obviously hero-worshipped her brothers, she was also amused by Leo and his odd ways. What emerges from her stories about him is a child who is always quite sure he knows best, and who is determined to succeed in anything he undertakes. Once, he airily announced he would run behind the carriage all the way on its journey to town – 'nothing easier' – and Masha remembered him having to be hauled into the carriage almost dead with exhaustion. Another time he nearly drowned in a pond which he insisted on claiming was only a foot deep. After these débâcles the little boy would never explain or apologize but remained as obstinate and self-willed as ever.

Nothing like this is mentioned in *Childhood*, and this is perhaps significant. Like many writers of piercing insight, into themselves as well as others, Tolstoy had his own blind spots: aspects of himself – the primacy of his own will in this case – which it never occurred to him to notice. From *Childhood* onwards all his heroes tend to be passive: always seeking for something but inclined to be acted upon rather than acting. The man who created them was certainly never like that. He was always determined to do and to get what he wanted.

His father died in 1837, seven years after his wife's death, and the young Tolstoys found themselves orphans, looked after first by their grandmother and afterwards by the beloved Aunt Tatiana, the greatest source of affection and comfort for Tolstoy during his young manhood and earlier. (There is an odd parallel with Pushkin, whose old nurse played the same role in his life, since the poet never had any feeling for his mother and father.) Tolstoy embarked on the desultory existence of a young man about town, almost for a time becoming the Russian 'superfluous man', like Pushkin's Eugene Onegin, and his own youthful Pierre at the beginning of *War and Peace*. Such a man, with plenty of money and all the social privileges of rank in a deeply deferential and hierarchic society, could hardly help being spoilt, as well as finding nothing to do, and nothing to exercise whatever true talents he might possess. During this period the young Tolstoy becomes obsessed for a time with the niceties of social behaviour, and with what is *comme il faut* – should he wear yellow or brown gloves? – did the best people ignore church-going, wear English shirts, join the army? – the sort of preoccupations that jostle in the head of an intensely curious, competitive and self-conscious young man.

He tries going to Kazan university, reads various subjects – law, mathematics, Russian literature – soon gives it up. He begins to keep a diary, in which he makes endless rules of behaviour for himself, rules which he continually breaks, goes back on, and revises again and again. For this compulsive self-scrutiny and rule-making does not stop him gambling, going to brothels, and wasting his time and money with dashing young men. And yet he never really let himself go, retaining always a certain wariness and sense of self-preservation; a sense, too, of basic dislike of the way he and the others were living, and a determination to do and to be something different.

Those 'Rules for Life' which he was always drawing up, and then failing of course to adhere to, are one indication of this; another is the extreme restlessness with which he tries one thing after another, failing always to satisfy himself that he has found the one true and proper course of life. Yet always, even at this disheartening and aimless period, a secret but passionate intention to make a name for himself by writing is always there. He even begins to compose an experimental story, to be called 'A History of Yesterday', and which is just that. Although it soon peters out, it already shows many of the unique characteristics of Tolstoy's later style: literalness pursued almost to the point of verbal clumsiness, and a deceptive air of simplicity.

Yasnaya Polyana, the house where he had been born, was settled on Tolstoy as his share of the paternal estates – it comprised 4,000 acres and 350 serfs – and he now began to live there, still in considerable embarrassment from gambling debts and other liabilities. His beloved aunt came to keep house for him; he started a school and began the idea of writing the book that became *Childhood;* but very soon he gave it up, and on an impulse decided to follow his brother Nikolai, of whom he was very fond, to the Caucasus. The beginning of this journey is most vividly described in the opening of what is in a sense his first true novel, *The Cossacks*.

Nikolai was an artillery officer, and Tolstoy was soon persuaded to take some simple exams and to follow his brother into the army. The artillery was the élite corps in the Russian forces, and Tolstoy remained very proud of them and of his days as a cadet and junior officer. The artillery captain Tushin is the modest and highly competent hero in the description of the battle of Borodino in *War and Peace*. Tolstoy himself behaved bravely under fire in several encounters with the local Chechen tribesmen, and he afterwards looked back on his two and a half years in the Caucasus as the happiest in his life. He enjoyed the disciplined idleness of army routine, the comradeship of his fellows, and the opportunities he had for writing and thinking. He completed *Childhood*, and sent it off to Nekrasov, the editor of a progressive periodical *The Contemporary*, which had originally been started by Pushkin.

Nekrasov liked the story, much to Tolstoy's delight, and it was admired too by Turgenev, already a famous writer, and also by Dostoevsky in distant Siberia, who acquired a copy of the magazine and wrote to ask a friend 'who was the mysterious L.N?' 'A new and remarkable talent' was the conclusion of one reviewer. Tolstoy's most cherished ambition seemed about to be realized; and although he had fits of self-doubt, as well as of remorse and misery for his continued gambling and womanizing, he had found a rich field for exploring his own individuality as a writer. Before he left the Caucasus at the end of 1853 he had written several stories, including the marvellous sketch called 'The Woodfelling', and these in their way are as good as anything he ever wrote. He also continued with the story of *Boyhood* and planned other projects, including what was to become *The Cossacks*.

Early in 1854 the Crimean war broke out, and he requested a transfer to the front. His service in the Crimea showed his usual bravery under fire, but he was lucky too; for high-placed relatives, and the Tsar himself, requested that he should be posted away from the most dangerous bastions in Sevastopol, where he would almost certainly have been killed. His disgust with the mass bloodshed of modern war, so different from the more gentlemanly and sporting skirmishes in the Caucasus, made him quite ready to acquiesce in this. The Crimea could be said to have turned him from a normal young Russian taking pleasure in his country's imperial expansion into an ardent pacifist; although he always retained his admiration for the simple soldier, and at the very end of his life, when the Japanese were besieging Port Arthur, he swore that he himself, and the soldiers of his own time, would never have given the place up.

More significant, perhaps, when we read accounts of his life and feelings at the time, is the way Tolstoy could hardly help taking for granted his own extraordinarily privileged position in society, and in the Russia of his class and period. Nothing quite like that combination of social prestige and irresponsibility would have been possible elsewhere in Europe then, or among societies and communities since. Tolstoy could do as he pleased; he even had the ear of the Tsar, when he wrote protesting not against the war itself but against the inhuman conditions in which the soldiers at the battlefront had to live. And the tales he was rapidly writing about his Crimean experiences were already making him famous. None the less he was also already beginning to feel dissatisfied, detached from his friends and his country, unable to submerge himself wholly in their interests and way of life. He was beginning to experience the loneliness of the seeker after a truth of his own, and the sort of guilt that went with a clear knowledge of his own status and talents and advantages.

He also began to want to settle down. Back at Yasnaya Polyana he took to visiting neighbours, the Arsenevs, whose eldest daughter Valerya attracted him. It was this romance that was to produce the novella *Family Happiness*, a touching and beautifully written piece with which Tolstoy himself none the less always remained dissatisfied. This was perhaps because its happy ending seemed to him too glib; and it was certainly unlike any 'ending' that his own turbulent domestic life could ever have afforded.

In any case he soon tired of poor Valerya, all the more so perhaps because he had now contracted a steady affair with a pretty married serf called Aksinya Bazykin. He had had several seigneurial raids on his peasant girls before, but this was something more serious, although it soon became filled with his usual revulsion, loathing and self-disgust where his own sexual experience was concerned. His diary of the period is unusually vivid however. 'Today, in the big old woods. I'm a fool, a brute. Her bronze flush and her eyes ... I'm in love as never before in my life.' From this liaison there was born a son, who probably lived most of his life on the estate. Tolstoy of course confided all the details of these local love affairs to his diary, together with all his feelings of lust, guilt and remorse – the remorse that he was later to give to the hero of his novel *Resurrection*. When he subsequently became engaged he insisted that his future wife should read his diaries, and she was predictably horrified and shocked. Perhaps Tolstoy intended her to be. Like most men he had a streak of Don Juan in his make-up; and his desire for total honesty had something a touch theatrical about it, as such desires often have. Besides, the Sophie Behrs whom he married was a tough young woman, however sheltered the life which her class and the conventions of the time had compelled her to lead, and it may well be that she was not so shocked as he supposed her to be. No doubt her future husband would have been shocked himself if she had not seemed to be. None the less, the episode planted the seeds of suspicion, jealousy and resentment which were to torment them both in middle age, and lead to that extraordinary rivalry of the diaries – his and hers – which was one of the most dramatic and also sadly and comically touching aspects of their later life together.

His restlessness at this time drove Tolstoy to Europe, where he visited Paris, Switzerland and, briefly, London. One object was to see his brother Nikolai, who was being treated in Germany for tuberculosis. His brother's death upset him greatly, and gave him his first experience of that horror of death that was to appear later in *Anna Karenina*, and in the story *The Death of Ivan Ilyich*. But as Andrew Wilson has pointed out in his excellent modern life of Tolstoy, this fear of death was itself an aspect of the great writer's remarkable aliveness, and extra-keen sense of the flesh. 'The Seer of the Flesh' the nineteenth-century Russian critic Merezhkovsky was to call him as opposed to Dostoevsky, 'the Seer of the Spirit'. Wilson dryly records that at the time of his brother's actual death Tolstoy was in fact leading a highly social life in the capital, attending soirées and court balls, and that he failed to abandon the delights of the season to attend his brother in his last illness.

This demonstrates one of the many paradoxes of Tolstoy's life, and the one that was to cause him most self-reproach. His greatness as a writer came precisely from his quite unusual power of personifying contradictions. He loved 'society' and he hated it. He believed in pacifism and non-resistance, but could himself be the most arrogant and quarrelsome of men. He was in every way a profound conservative, and yet he was sure that the future must be transformed by a whole new philosophy of peace, progress and love. Towards the end of his life these contradictions assume touching forms. At a time when he insisted on dressing like a peasant, living on porridge and vegetables, making his own boots (very badly) and emptying his own chamber-pot, he used to ask avidly of his daughters about the fashions among the young beauties of St Petersburg, and what court dresses were being worn. Nothing is more decisively human in the writer and his work than this endless questioning and dissatisfaction, combined with a passionate love of things as they actually were.

Dogmatic as he always was, he can continually surprise us, both in his works and in his notes and diaries, by sudden flashes of penetrating reasonableness and common sense. Sometimes these can seem almost banal, and a surprise to Tolstoy himself, as when he notes after a vigorous argument with a scholar in science and religion that 'Christ did not impose but revealed a moral law that will always remain a standard of good and evil'. That comment may remind the reader of Levin's perplexity in *Anna Karenina*, when after a prolonged and sterile discussion with some intellectual friends he has a sudden revelation from the old gardener, who speaks in a simple innocent way about those who live rightly. The secret seems revealed: but then it goes again, and we are back in the mire of self-doubts, questionings, and attempts to arrive at truth through new ideas and intellectual debate. Quoting the pre-Socratic Greek proverb about 'the fox who knows many things while the tortoise knows one big thing', Isaiah Berlin brilliantly summed up Tolstoy's predicament as that of a fox who was striving always to be a hedgehog. Tolstoy's pitiless common sense could only tell him that man lives in and on an endless plurality of contradiction and variety, but his yearning for truth convinced him that the great simple solution must exist, or must be made to exist.

In 1855 his writing was temporarily at a standstill. Although he had become well known as a Russian writer, principally through the popularity of his *Sebastopol Sketches,* he had managed to alienate the literati of St Petersburg, including Turgenev, and his more recent stories had not been well received. Despite its wonderful descriptive charm, *Family Happiness* contains all Tolstoy's most dogmatic assertions about the nature of love, and a woman's duty in love; and it was no wonder that the pitilessly self-perceiving side of him said it was no good, a dishonest abomination: he even tried, too late, to cancel its publication. He thought he was through as a writer, and made this revealing comment in his diary. 'Temptation through vanity. I could gain much in life if I wished to write without conviction'. But he promptly adds: 'My only and chief occupation... must be literature. My aim is literary fame, the good that I can accomplish by my writing.' That in itself is typically Tolstoyan – the barefaced way he puts two such propositions together without further comment. He wants to be famous and he wants to do good. Not for nothing did Tolstoy come from a long line of crafty diplomats, accustomed to hearing and uttering hypocrisy with an immovable face.

Yet it is probably true that at this particularly perplexed and tormented period of his life Tolstoy might have abandoned writing altogether, out of disgust with himself and with what a later generation of intellectuals would call the *mauvaise foi* of literature. His story written in Switzerland, 'Lucerne', is by his own harsh standards as dishonest as *Family Happiness*. In protesting against a social injustice – the unfeelingness shown by some gentlefolk to a streetplayer – it protests too much to sound quite natural, and to achieve the true inevitability of art. More effective and more interesting is the story of the same period called 'Two Hussars', which describes with graphic effectiveness the difference between an officer of the old school – a rake, gambler and womanizer, but generous and holding instinctive ideas of honour – with his cold-hearted young modern counterpart. This story may indeed be more interesting even than its lively structure and detail reveal; for in a curious way it looks forward to the real purpose and meaning behind *War and Peace*. Tolstoy the conservative had begun to detest the radical and progressive movements and personalities of the time, with their emphasis on abstract ideology and wholesale 'reform'; and he had begun increasingly to look back on the values of the past, and what the gentry class in Russia had achieved.

There is a close connection, too, between the inception of *War and Peace* and Tolstoy's marriage. Quite suddenly, as he noted in his diary, it had become easier to live, easier to write, and to think. All this he owed, and unconsciously for the most part, to his young wife, whom he married in 1862, and with whom he went at once to live in the country. From then on, whatever the storms and stresses of the marriage, and his own hidden or open exasperation with family life, he had a way to live, and a means of reconciling those contradictory sides of his nature that were always at war within him. *War and Peace* was the greatest expression of his conservative side, a labour of love and, in a sense too, of farewell, to his own class and to its role in Russia's history. The war, and the peace, were inside him, and from now on the first was to predominate.

Tolstoy spent more than five years working on *War and Peace* while his young family was being born and brought up, and it was probably the happiest time of his life. His schoolmasterly instincts were still very much to the fore, and he exercised them not only on his own young children but also in the local school he had set up, which was to occupy more and more of his time and interest. Like many born teachers he was arrogant, and convinced that he was always right – we can see in this the same little boy who nearly drowned rather than admit a pond was more than a foot deep – but he had a tremendous gaiety of spirit when with the very young, and many of his pupils remembered all their lives the intoxicating pleasure of being taught by him. 'There am I,' wrote one of them, 'a ten-year-old schoolboy, romping with young jolly Leo Nicolayevich, sliding down the steep hill, covering him with snow, walking with him in the woods and fields, and having talks on the terrace.' This ability to transform people's lives and 'make souls burn more brightly' was of course the secret of Tolstoy's tremendous later magnetism among 'Tolstoyans' – those who uncritically accepted all the teachings, sometimes cranky ones, of his later years. But the vision of the young man playing with and teaching children is in a sense a far cry from the tormented egocentric he was later to become. His vigorous Russian spontaneity and sense of the fullness of life overflowed during his best years, not only into his work but into the whole of his daily existence.

After *War and Peace* was finished there came an inevitable anticlimax. Tolstoy taught himself ancient Greek – quite an achievement for a man in his 40s – and busied himself yet more intensively with his educational projects. In his typically high-handed manner he demanded of the officials at the Ministry of Education their study of his own plan for comprehensive changes in school-teaching, and his separate plan for training the teachers. The Ministry naturally delayed and raised objections, but at last in 1878 gave its authorization for a teachers' training seminary at

Yasnaya Polyana. The result, unfortunately, was another anticlimax. Although Tolstoy had renovated and rebuilt part of his manor house to provide classrooms for the pupils, only a dozen or so enrolled themselves in what he had thought of as his new 'university of best shoes'. His school for the very young had been a different class of thing altogether. But it may well be that more mature students were intimidated not only by the overwhelming personality of the great man himself but by the knowledge – as omnipresent in Tsarist as in Soviet Russia – that the scheme might not have the government's full approval.

However it was, Tolstoy himself lost interest. Like most masterful people, he was inclined to abandon any scheme which he could not dominate wholly himself, and he turned to other matters and other crusades, though he never regretted time spent teaching and continued until his last years to instruct small children round the estate who showed interest and promise. But not for nothing was the figure of Goethe's Faust, the restless and never satisfied seeker, a dominant image for the nineteenth-century intellectual. Unless it was continually occupied the powerful mechanism of Tolstoy's mind and spirit would soon begin to consume itself, and to end in despair; he had no capacity to recognize and respond to the teachings of Buddha or the tranquillities of eastern religion. Quite suddenly, when on a business journey to Arzamas, he suffered an appalling attack of fear and horror which he referred to afterwards as the Arzamas experience. A total personal and spiritual vacuum overwhelmed him, and a sense of the finality of death, so terrible that nothing he had done in life seemed worth bothering about.

A lot of people have such a crisis and get over it, more or less, and usually in silence. For Tolstoy, of course, it had to be the occasion for the proclamation of a new gospel, a new and definitive personal statement. As the excellent Russian critic and historian Prince Mirsky puts it, 'from henceforward Tolstoy ceased to be a writer, in the sense of a man who writes for the sake of producing good literary work, and became a preacher'. In fact his crisis had occurred while he was still working on *Anna Karenina*, of which, though he began it with high hopes, he tired before the end, lamenting the need to drag himself back to 'dull old Anna'. Nothing could have been more indicative of the change in his life and attitudes than Tolstoy's virtual rejection, even before he completed it, of this marvellously diverse and densely populated work of fiction (it contains as many as 140 characters) with its air of 'living life' in all its many manifestations continuing and justifying itself to the end (Anna's last reflection, almost, is about a joke she thinks she will tell her lover).

But so it was; and the great writer embarked on a new career as a seer and preacher, roles which had always been implicit in his previous authoritarian outlook, but were now to be concealed under the guise of meekness, humility, and obedience to God's law. Between 1880 and 1883 Tolstoy wrote *A Confession*, a remarkable work in a new, plain and oratorical style which set out his new creed and new convictions. After his crisis he had turned first to the Orthodox church, but had soon become convinced that a simpler and more basic Christian creed was required. This departure further alienated him from the Countess Tolstoy, and there began the sad process of estrangement which only ended at Astapovo railway station, after Tolstoy had fled from his home at the age of 82, in 1910.

It was a tragedy, but also a tragicomedy, whose grievously absurd and yet comically touching side the Tolstoy of earlier years would have been well able to appreciate, for in his own curious way he had a great sense of humour. It is touching, too, to think of those two old people, wife and husband, solemnly exchanging their diaries, in order to read the extremely unfavourable things each had written about the other. And it is revealing, though in a more macabre way, that one of the last 'friends', on whom Tolstoy thought he could depend, should have been the sinister Chertkov, an ex-Guards Officer who came from the same aristocratic background as Tolstoy himself. Sophia Tolstoy not unnaturally hated Chertkov, and did everything she possibly could to frustrate his attempts to get the fortune that was to be made from the great writer's literary assets into his own hands, for the benefit of 'the cause'. In this he was at least partially successful, for the sons and daughters were divided against each other, some at least supporting their mother in her wish to keep the family fortune in her own hands.

It was this misery that finally drove the great writer from the house where he had been born. He had long cherished the dream of setting out alone as a pilgrim, one of the 'Fools of Christ' who wandered the roads of Russia, blessing the simple folk and living on their alms. He had marvellously described such people in *Childhood,* and the impression they had made on the young narrator and his sister. Now he determined to become one himself. But like all such dreams of ideal living this one ended in anticlimax, as the Tolstoy who wrote *Anna Karenina,* and *The Death of Ivan Ilyich,* would have well known that it must. His wife was soon with him again; and though he refused to see her she prowled round the station-master's tiny house, begging and complaining. Her lot had become as pathetic as his own.

As is the way with official legends of great men, his followers were told that his last words were: 'To seek – always to seek'. Perhaps they were, but his favourite daughter, who had remained devoted to him, always remembered his saying to her like a small anxious child: 'I do not understand what it is I have to do.' And he now needed do nothing but die.

In all Russia and around the world the news of his death brought shock and grief. Like Queen Victoria in England he had been an institution going far back in the public memory, and his passing seemed the end of an entire age. The Russian novelist Nabokov, a child at the time, remembered his father sitting in a deckchair with a newspaper in his hand, and turning to say to his wife, *'Tiens, Tolstoy vient de mourir'*. The pair said nothing more, recalled the young Nabokov, but sat in silence. Gorky, when he heard the news, said that Tolstoy and death had been like two bears in one den, and that he had somehow taken for granted that Tolstoy was the stronger.

He was buried in the deep old wood at Yasnaya Polyana, at 'the place of the green stick'. When they were children his brother Nikolai had buried there a sliver of fresh sapling which he told his brothers had magical properties, and would one day save the world and make everything in it holy and beautiful. The child Leo had devoutly believed this, and he never forgot the moment, or the spot where it had taken place. The site of the burial is now visited every year by thousands of tourists, and by Tolstoyans making their pilgrimage to the writer's home.

2

War and Peace

Most great novels succeed in terms of their complete individuality. They seem free in a very special sense – free of fashion and intention, free even of the conditions under which they were composed. *War and Peace* appears as a supreme example of this freedom, and some comments by the author show why this is so, surprising – even rather shocking – as they are.

> Those Englishmen who come to Russia feel much more free here. At home they are bound by laws they make themselves... and which they obey, imagining they are free men. Now in this country it was not I who made the laws, so I am not bound to obey them – I am the free man.

We might raise our eyebrows at this descendant of so many aristocratic diplomats shamelessly expounding so equivocal a doctrine. Is this the casuistry, the bottomless cynicism, which Conrad the novelist says is in the politics of the Russian soul? Perhaps it is, and yet the freedom which Tolstoy enjoyed as a privileged gentleman under the Tsarist system is undeniable. No *War and Peace* could have been written under the Soviet system: any equivalent would either have been conformist, or it would have been secret and rebellious; and it is the great strength of *War and Peace* that it is neither, and needs to be neither.

Tolstoy once said that he had learnt from the French novelist Stendhal how to describe war. What had struck him, as it has struck many more recent readers, for Stendhal's novels caused no great stir in their own time, was the way the Frenchman had recognized and described the fragmentary banality which is all the experience the average individual has of battle. Stendhal's hero is never afterwards sure whether he has been at the battle of Waterloo or not, for everything that happened to him that day, however sickening or frightening, seemed also quite fragmentary and inconclusive.

Tolstoy frees, so to speak, Stendhal's shoulder-shrugging and offhand perception and gives it the whole wide perspective of his panoramic vision. In his early accounts of military action, in the Caucasus and the Crimea, he had demonstrated very effectively the homeliness of the military life, and the way in which soldiers pass their time, even in situations of danger. Habit makes them continue to smoke and chat even when bullets or cannonballs are whistling about. Only the young and idealistic see warfare in a preconceived manner, with everything taking place as it should, or as it is supposed to. Tolstoy gives a good example of this in the short novel *The Cossacks*, whose hero Olenin is a prototype of all the naïve and opinionated young men we shall meet in Tolstoy's later accounts of warfare. A comic idealist, Olenin thinks he knows just how the Chechen tribesmen – *abreks* as they are called – will behave.

> Olenin was very much impressed by the place in which the *abreks* lay. In fact it was very much like the rest of the steppe, but because the *abreks* were there it seemed to detach itself from all the rest and become distinguished. Indeed it appeared to Olenin the very place for *abreks* to occupy.

There are much wider implications in this demonstration that Tolstoy makes so frequently. Most of us go through life with a preconceived notion of things, moving, as it were, on the predestined path for which normal consciousness has fitted us. Tolstoyan freedom enlarges the whole possibility of vision and awareness by showing, in big ways and in small, how immensely wide and various and unpredictable everything is. Olenin is convinced that his tribesmen are behaving according to plan, the preconceived plan that exists in his own head. He will soon be shown to be wrong.

It is for reasons like these that Tolstoy has been called the greatest of writers about war. But his experience of war works as part of his wider method: the operation of 'making it strange'. Everything we find, see, and feel in *War and Peace* has been defamiliarized by the author's method and vision, which is all the stranger because the great book itself, as we get into it, begins to seem more and more familiar, as if we had always known the things that it was showing and telling us. But the explanation for this paradox is simple. Tolstoy is giving us the freedom that is indeed continually on the borders of our consciousness, which daily habit and routine cause us most of the time to ignore. But it is there, and we do know about it, and Tolstoy suddenly makes us free of it in ways that no other writer quite does, or can do.

Some of the explanations for this unique sense of space and freedom are, as it were, quite mechanical ones. The peculiar conditions of Russia at the time were themselves a great help to Tolstoy's method. Huge and primitive as the country was, the upper class who ran it was comparatively small, and formed almost a kind of club or association, most of the members of which knew each other. Without that combination of *size* and *intimacy* the enormous wheels of *War and Peace* could hardly continue to revolve. Tolstoy in fact borrowed from Sir Walter Scott the ancient literary device of coincidence, in which daughters suddenly encounter their mothers in the Arabian desert, or fathers their long-lost sons in a Scottish shipwreck. Tolstoy naturalizes it of course by seeming to take it for granted; and it is interesting in this connection that a distinguished descendant of his great novel – Pasternak's *Dr Zhivago* – uses coincidence as a quasi-symbolic method, to illustrate the chaos brought about by the revolution, and the ways in which members of a family would vanish from one day to the next, and then be reunited months or even years later.

Tolstoy's traditional use of the device is illustrated by some classic instances, such as Princess Mary's rescue from threatening peasants by Nicholas Rostov, whom she will subsequently marry, and the liberation of Pierre from the retreating French army by his old rival Dolokhov, with whom he had once fought a duel. Halfway through the novel we are casually told, in Tolstoy's offhand way, that Pierre 'knew everyone in Moscow and St Petersburg'. The grand cocktail party with which the novel opens silently illustrates the same sort of social principle, and the first words spoken by Princess Anna Scherer give a whole structure its tone.

It may seem a frivolous tone, but the author is not in the least bothered by this sort of social frivolity, he knows that this is how great events proceed and are talked about, in terms of gossip and intrigue by often quite trivial individuals. There is nothing 'idealistic' about the society which Tolstoy presents: self-interest and class interest are what matter, but in time of the crisis of nations these are the very things that can give a society cohesion, and help to save the country. When the Rostov family are trying to get their goods out of the city as the French are threatening Moscow, the wounded are lying about waiting to be evacuated, and there is a shortage of carts. Which will be saved – the Rostovs' goods or the wounded soldiers? It is an interesting case where Tolstoy's method steers rather close to the wind in presenting class good as public good, for Natasha Rostov indignantly protests that the wounded must be put in the carts ('Are we Germans or something?') and yet in some way there is room both for the grand family's possessions and for the casualties of war as well.

There are moments when Tolstoy seems almost consciously to draw the reader's attention to the class solidarity he so deeply if almost unconsciously accepted at the time he wrote the novel. An engaging example occurs when Nicholas Rostov's friend and fellow officer Colonel Denisov, who was based on the real-life leader Davydov, goes to the Russian commander in chief with a plan for attacking the French.

> 'I give my word of honour as a Russian Officer,' said Denisov, 'that I can break Napoleon's line of communication.'
> 'What relation are you to Intendant-General Kiril Andreevich Denisov?' asked Kutuzov, interrupting him.
> 'He is my uncle, your Serene Highness.'
> 'Ah, we were friends,' said Kutuzov cordially.

In one of the introductions that he wrote for the parts of the novel as they came out Tolstoy remarked that he was ignorant of the lives of priests and students and merchants, and only familiar with the lives of the gentry class, which he knew and loved. Such honesty may sound arrogant today, but it came quite naturally to Tolstoy, who strongly – if again almost unconsciously – believed in the solidarity of the gentry with the peasants, and the mutual understanding between the two. We can hardly understand the background of *War and Peace* without realizing that it was written not only as a kind of celebration of the way in which gentry and peasants together had fought off the invader fifty years before, but as a statement about the problems that had arisen in the sixties with the liberation of the peasants from serfdom, and the consequent troubles between masters and men. Tolstoy had seen a good deal on his own estate, and felt that the traditional relations of the two classes could and should continue, on a basis of mutual help and esteem – just the kind of solidarity in the face of troubles that he felt had been shown by peasants and gentry in 1812.

It is significant that the first tentative drafts of the novel carried the provisional title 'All's Well that Ends Well'. The title of a Shakespearean comedy seems a peculiar one for Tolstoy to have chosen, but there seems no doubt that he thought of the work as a kind of transcendent comedy, covering space and time, life and death, war and peace. It asserted life, and the simplicities of life, and hence could not fail to be hopeful, in the way that Natasha Rostov, the most significant vessel of life and vitality, cannot help being hopeful. She knows that life will use her, must use her, for its own purposes, and is unthinkingly joyful at the prospect. Even when she is betrothed to a dying man, Prince Andrew, she is convinced he will recover and live, because that is what she herself so much wants and needs. The pair converse when the prince is lying wounded.

> 'Shall I live? What do you think?
> 'I am sure of it – sure!' Natasha almost shouted, taking hold of both of his hands in a passionate moment.

Even after Prince Andrew has died Natasha, the involuntary vessel of life, is convinced that he must still be alive somewhere. 'Where is he and who is he now?' she demands – a query weakened in the standard English translation, which cannot quite face the literalness of the Russian *kto* – 'who'.

In *What is Art?*, the in many ways perverse pamphlet that Tolstoy wrote much later in life, after his dogmatic convictions had hardened, he none the less asked the question that the great world of *War and Peace* seems destined to answer.

> What can be older than the relations of married couples, of parents to children, of children to parents; the relations of men to their fellow-countrymen, and to foreigners, to an invasion, to a defence, to property, to the land?

By the time he wrote *What is Art?* Tolstoy was convinced that art itself, in the usual sense, was a sham, and that its validity resided only in the simplicity and universality of its operation. Tolstoy illustrated this by the example of a Vogul wolf-hunt, when the tribesmen afterwards would gather round and enact the events they had taken part in. This he felt was what real art was about – certainly not the linguistic elaboration of Shakespeare, or that of modern authors and novelists.

Although Tolstoy had by then repudiated his own novels, and all his work except the didactic stories, there is a curious sense in which *War and Peace* is in fact fulfilling the very functions which its author later came to feel were the only point of art. *War and Peace is* simple, universal, and almost immediate in its effect upon everyone who opens it. What Tolstoy later ignored, of course, was the simple fact that simple people are not in the least put off by sophisticated goings-on in courts and among kings, princes, and grandees. On the contrary, they love to hear about such things; and, as he himself puts it in relation to marriage talk and to conversation among children and peasants, each person understands things in his own way. Tolstoy first thought of calling old Count Rostov, the patriarch of the novel, Count Prostoy, the 'simple', or the honest straightforward one. The didactic idea behind that was not really necessary, for Rostov, with all his faults and weaknesses, does indeed invisibly appear as a kind of hallmark of values which any reader from any background could recognize.

This simplicity can, as it were, swallow up any quantity of sophistication in the way the fiction and its events are planned and organized. 'Anyone writing a novel', says Tolstoy in a later essay on Guy de Maupassant, a French novelist he thought talented but immoral, and whose outlook he despised, 'must have a clear and firm idea as to what is good and bad in life.' That may seem self-evident when we come to think of it, and yet it is a point of real importance none the less. Anyone reading a fairy-story knows what is good and bad in its characters, and the same is true of *War and Peace,* but with a big difference. Everyone in Tolstoy's novel has their own individuality, which in a sense is neither good nor bad but simply their own. Judgements there are of course, but they do not affect the individuals' nature, and their inalienable right, as it were, to be themselves. This fact is borne in on Prince Andrew, himself a somewhat severe and didactic personage, when, on the retreat during the summer of 1812 through the Russian countryside with his regiment, he sees in the confusion of his country estate, from which the serfs and farmers are fleeing, two little girls engaged in stealing plums:

> ... two little girls, running out of the hot-house carrying in their skirts plums they had plucked from the trees there, came upon Prince Andrew. On seeing the young master the elder one, with frightened look, clutched her younger companion by the hand, and hid with her behind a birch tree, not stopping to pick up some green plums that they had dropped.
>
> Prince Andrew turned away with startled haste, unwilling to let them see that they had been observed. He was sorry for the pretty frightened little girl, was afraid of looking at her, and yet felt an irresistible desire to do so. A new sensation of comfort and relief came over him when, seeing these girls, he realised the existence of other human interests entirely aloof from his own, and just as legitimate as those that occupied him. Evidently those girls passionately desired one thing – to carry away and eat those green plums without being caught – and Prince Andrew shared their wish for the success of their enterprise. He could not resist looking at them once more... Believing their danger past, they sprang from their ambush, and chirruping something in their shrill little voices and holding up their skirts, their bare little sunburned feet scampered lively and quick across the meadow grass.

The marvellous passage shows exactly in miniature what the great book shows as a whole: that everyone has their own business and attends to it in their own way. What is good and bad in life coexists with what is of its own nature, and continues as such, come what may. Again and again this truth is displayed, not as it seems by Tolstoy himself but by the logic and the imagination of the work.

Anatoly Kuragin, for example, is a most undesirable character, a rake and a seducer, who would have done his best to ruin Natasha, tempted as she is by his desire, and by her own. But the picture of Kuragin that Tolstoy shows us is that of a person who is none the less unique as an individual and absolutely content to be himself.

> Anatoly was not quick-witted, nor ready or eloquent in conversation, but he had the faculty, so invaluable in society, of composure and imperturbable self-possession. If a man lacking in self-confidence remains dumb on a first introduction, and betrays a consciousness of the impropriety of such silence, the effect is bad. But Anatoly was dumb, swung his foot, and smilingly examined the Princess's hair. It was evident that he could be silent in this way for a very long time. 'If anyone finds this silence inconvenient, let him talk, but I don't want to,' he seemed to say.

Most of the huge cast of *War and Peace* become vividly present to us through this uncanny ability of Tolstoy's to suggest the whole of an individual, no matter how unimportant he or she may be to the action, by means of these flickers of intimacy he gives us of individuals. Whether they are the little girls stealing plums in the orchard or Anatoly courting the Princess Mary, they are revealed in all the mystery of their own purposes and their own selves. The critic Shklovsky's famous comment about Tolstoy's way of 'making it strange' could be said to apply with an even greater force to his way of making strangers and passers-by in the novel suddenly familiar.

And such vividness is of course all the more immediate and striking when it is applied to a character who is well known historically, like Napoleon himself, or one to whom the reader has been introduced as a famous actor in the panorama, like the Russian general Bagration. Tolstoy's secret here is, significantly, to see such an important figure as if he were physically fresh and new, like a boy, almost like a child. Napoleon at the battle of Austerlitz, the hour of his greatest triumph, has a face that 'wore that special look of confident, self-complacent happiness that one sees on the face of a boy happily in love'. And as he and his troops are going into action Bagration has the absolutely satisfied, concentrated look of a man on a hot day, who takes a little run before plunging into cool water.

This can be seen as a trick of Tolstoy's, as it has been considered by one or two of the more candid and less sympathetic of his Russian critics. Turgenev chided him for spending too much time on telling the reader how one of his characters held his left hand; and a later critic accused him of an odd new form of physical and psychological eavesdropping. But with Tolstoy there is always a special point in descriptions of this sort. Tolstoy the psychologist perceives that most of us have a kind of innate, unconscious, and inevitable satisfaction in being ourselves (in Russian, *samodovolstvo* or *samodovolnost*) which not only keeps us going from day to day, but which is involuntarily on view, in its various forms and manifestations, to anyone who is sharp enough or interested enough to pay real attention to the ways in which we behave. As used, and as delineated, by Tolstoy, the Russian term does not necessarily convey the same criticism that would be suggested by terms like 'self-satisfaction' and 'complacency'. Where Napoleon himself is concerned, or the Rostovs' partly German son-in-law Berg, the term may indeed be a pejorative one; and yet it is a quality which all reasonably happy and adjusted people possess, and which societies, communities, families above all, require for their harmonious working. Happy families have indeed all the same kinds of self-confidence.

The state of *samodovolnost* – happy and physical self-sufficiency – is quite compatible with the mentality of the seeker. Pierre has it, but Prince Andrew does not; and it is the source of the difficulties he finds in getting on with ordinary life, and with women like his wife, the Little Princess. She herself has a vibrantly joyous and sociable physicality, epitomized by the dark down on her upper lip and the way her graceful little nostrils seem to dilate when, like a warhorse, she scents from afar the world of balls and fashions. But she has a temperament disastrously incompatible with that of her husband. Her pathetic and touching death in childbirth is for him just one of the misfortunes which his own difficult and fastidious nature has in some way helped to bring about.

No simple pattern of contrasts will of course do justice to the complex and diverse world of *War and Peace*, although, as we shall see, it is more obviously evident in the structure of *Anna Karenina*. But it would not be untrue to suggest, none the less, that as well as war and peace we have in the growth and scope of the novel the twin worlds of life and death, and the significance that they suggest in human affairs and individualities. Andrew is made for death, Pierre for life; and of course it will happen that Natasha, the supreme vessel of life, will be for Pierre and not for Andrew. As early as *Childhood* Tolstoy makes this peculiarly physical apprehension of death and life a part of the composition of memory and being, as if the consciousness – and especially a consciousness in creating words – could experience them both simultaneously. The death of the narrator's mother in *Childhood* is followed by his apprehension of death at her funeral, when Tolstoy – borrowing from Dickens's *David Copperfield*, a book he much admired – makes his narrator not only acutely conscious of the aliveness produced in him by the proximity of death, and the death of one he so much loved, but aware that a special aspect of that aliveness is precisely the satisfaction he cannot help feeling in being so sad.

These 'patterns' in *War and Peace*, if we can call them that, are of an essentially different order from the purposeful and ideological organization to be found in the novella *Family Happiness*, in Tolstoy's late novels *Resurrection* and *The Kreutzer Sonata*, and in a powerful story like *The Death of Ivan Ilyich*. In all these examples the intention is evident and the didactic purpose clear, as it is also to some degree in *Anna Karenina*, although the complexity and multiformity of that great work magically equivocates its didacticism. In composing *Family Happiness* Tolstoy was not only aware of the schoolmasterish way in which his story had taken shape, but became disgusted with it. Later still, of course, and after the composition of *War and Peace*, he came to terms with the concept of art as social and spiritual polemic: something which his natural instincts as an artist were all against.

Those native instincts were never stronger than they were in the growth of the idea of *War and Peace*, and in the gradual planning of *Anna Karenina*. 'Family happiness' is one of the great topics of *War and Peace*, but unlike the earlier novella it has become not only a complex but an ambiguous and ruthless affair, involving loss and sacrifice as well as fulfilment. One of Tolstoy's most brilliant minor strokes is to show how one member of any close family is usually the misfit, not through any deliberate exclusion or hostility on the part of the others, but because he or she seems quite definitely a different sort of person. So it is in the Rostov family with Vera, whom even her mother finds perplexing and 'cannot think where she comes from'. Her character and being are just not those of the Rostovs, and they lead her to marriage with the dull but irreproachable Berg, who is somehow tedious and depressing to be with – guilt-inducing too, one intuits – just because, as his creator says, 'everything about him is so entirely satisfactory'.

If the elder sister Vera is not a true Rostov, neither of course is the Rostovs' cousin Sonya. Many readers have found it hard to forgive Tolstoy, or rather his favourite Natasha, for what seems in the end her condescending attitude to Sonya, whom she refers to as a 'barren flower'. Natasha, as a grown-up married woman, cannot help patronizing a woman without husband or children, and Tolstoy may seem here to be adding to Natasha's feeling the weight of his own conviction. Sonya was modelled to some extent on his own dear Aunt Tatiana, who had devoted herself to the care of a family without having children of her own. Sonya, as

Natasha perceives, is attached to the whole family and finds her fulfilment in being a part of it. And it may be as natural, implies Tolstoy, for some women to do this as for others to bear children. Sonya is not associated with death, like Andrew, or in a quite different way like Vera and Berg, but in her the life force takes a different form.

But there is still more to the family, and to family happiness, than this. Perhaps with a strange intuition of the role that his wife would in time be playing in protecting her family and its interests from the results of his own religious and pacifist convictions, and the dubious friends and connections they had brought into the family circle, Tolstoy shows us at the end of *War and Peace* how incompatible can be the demands of family life and the demands of the individual conscience. New problems are looming, and the two new families, those of Pierre and Natasha and Nicholas Rostov and the Princess Mary, confront them in their own different ways. For the first time the family itself, so powerfully and artfully celebrated in the whole movement of the work, now reveals itself in a more ambiguous dimension.

Not that Tolstoy ceases to celebrate it: on the contrary, all that it stands for seems more firmly in the ascendant than ever, although there is a sense of elegy, and of recollection too, as if the golden days of the old Rostovs will not be seen again. And of course they won't; but the younger generation is growing up, and Prince Andrew's son is already dreaming of doing something that will make his father and uncle Pierre 'proud of him', although in the dream that concludes the work his other uncle, Nicholas Rostov, has become a threatening figure, repressive and even tyrannical.

The family has been split, in fact. With an extraordinary creative diplomacy, almost unnoticeable among the harmonies, the great chords of music as E. M. Forster called them, which bring the movement of *War and Peace* to its close, Tolstoy – or rather, as it seems, the novel itself – shows that no harmonious synthesis but rather a new and challenging thesis and antithesis are rising out of time, place, and history. Tolstoy had read Hegel with profound attention, and had been deeply impressed by the philosophical picture of history he had drawn. He had also made a careful study of the period in Russia, only a few years before he was born, when the intelligentsia of the Russian upper class was full and fermenting with liberal hopes for the future. Those hopes had been dashed by the succession of Tsar Nicholas I, and the severity with which he had put down the liberal Decembrist movement, many of whose members had been sent to Siberia. Tolstoy's relatives had of course known those men; and he himself had seriously thought of writing a novel based on their experiences and their movement. Why he did not do so is not entirely clear, but we can perceive what may have been partly the reason in the concluding pages of *War and Peace* itself. Tolstoy's own explanation was that he found he could not understand or write about what happened in 1820, the year of the Decembrist revolt, unless he first thoroughly investigated the Napoleonic war that had preceded it, and the kind of class and individuals who had brought that war to a triumphant conclusion.

A truer reason for his not carrying out the project may have been that in investigating the history of the war years Tolstoy found himself drawing insensibly closer in spirit to the interests of his own class and kind. In the long run it was their power and influence which would have been, and was, threatened by the logic of their own liberalizing movement. In a brilliant exposition of the hidden politics of *War and Peace* the Russian-Jewish philosopher Shestov has shown how subtly equivocal is Tolstoy's own position as the book nears its end. In one way his position remains wholly consistent: he continues to support, through thick and thin, the demands of the family, the extended upper-class family of his own kind. Shestov shows how that family and its values are upheld not by the seeker Pierre, and the dead Prince Andrew with whom he had so close a relation, but by the much simpler and stupider figure of Nicholas, current representative of the old Rostov family, and by the spiritually 'superior' wife whom he adores, the Princess Mary. Shestov dryly draws our attention to the deadpan way in which Tolstoy outfaces an awkward situation, in the scene in which Mary tranquilly tells her husband that whatever the teachings of charity and religion may be, it is their duty to look after their own family, and to preserve its inheritance. Mary, in fact, is taking exactly the line that the Countess Tolstoy would take towards the end of Tolstoy's married life. Pierre himself may be on the verge of playing a heroic, or a quixotic, part, and facing exile in Siberia for his beliefs, in which case his wife Natasha would have certainly sacrificed all to accompany him. But for Nicholas and Mary their duty and their future is clear: they must cling to the conservative and family ideal, and to what they know and love and care for at home.

Tolstoy's own spiritual future is thus explicitly foreshadowed in *War and Peace*. His art could, in a sense, solve the tormenting problem which the pilgrimage of his life could not, for *War and Peace* leaves the problem unresolved, in the full aesthetic harmony of its close. Should we sacrifice ourselves and others on an endless quest for what is right and good? Or should we cherish our children and possessions around us, and cling to what we own and what our ancestors have bequeathed to us. Like Mary and Nicholas (whom Shestov refers to sardonically as the true hero and heroine of *War and Peace)* Tolstoy's deepest instincts were all for the latter way, but his reasoning conscience and intelligence plagued him endlessly to believe and to do otherwise. Never again, in his art, was he to find a natural and harmonious solution. In his later work, and in varying measure, he had to *assert* what he believed to be right, instead of allowing a natural process to make its own undercover revelation.

Had Tolstoy gone on to prolong *War and Peace*, as he once intended, and written a Part II to his already immense novel which would have described the sufferings of the Decembrists and their devoted wives in Siberia, the cat would, so to speak, have been out of the bag. He would have had to reveal openly where his own sympathies and convictions lay, and provide an exposition of them in the light of history, in the way that his literary descendant Solzhenitsyn was to do in *The Red Wheel*, which is a monumental post-mortem on the origins of the revolution and the Soviet state in the fatal disasters of the first world war. Enormous as it is, *War and Peace* breaks off when its symphonic pattern is completed and its shape determined, not by ideology or counter-ideology but by the lives of individuals and families, and their inter-reaction with the complex sequences of events in a vast country during an epic period in its history.

3

Anna Karenina

The photograph taken of Sub-Lieutenant Count Tolstoy in 1854, showing him in his dark artillery officer's uniform, the epaulet proudly displayed beside the sable collar of his cloak, might be taken as an image of the size, arrogance and power of the Russian empire. The curling side-whiskers, moustache, and bullet head, emphasize that famously penetrating stare, but in a wholly worldly and imperial context. This could almost be the terrible *kumir*, the Bronze Horseman of Pushkin's poem.

It could also almost be a likeness of Vronsky, the figure of power and glamour in *Anna Karenina*, who brings so much joyous exultation and inflicts so much damage, on himself and on the heroine. There is no doubt about Tolstoy's feeling for Vronsky – almost, it might be said, his nostalgia for him – as the kind of man he himself might once have been. Tolstoy despised and hated men like Napoleon, with their inhuman lust for conquest and power; but his secret affection for high-born men of action, generous in their ambitions and in their passions, remained undiminished with age, and perhaps even increased. Throughout the novel he emphasizes Vronsky's physicality, and his sense of himself, which though it is greatly enhanced by his love for Anna still remains separated from it. When the couple are happiest in their love the novel sees them alone and apart from each other. *We* never see them happy together, as we see the married couples at the end of *War and Peace*. At the time of the famous horse-race, when Vronsky's mare Frou-Frou breaks her back over a jump, Vronsky is incongruously happy, but he is happiest at the prospect of seeing Anna, not when he is actually with her. In his carriage he becomes conscious of the sprain he got in the accident.

> He put down his legs, threw one of them over the other, and placing his arm across it felt its firm calf, where he had hurt it in the fall the day

> before, and then, throwing himself back, sighed deeply several times.
>
> 'Delightful! O delightful!' he thought. He had often before been joyfully conscious of his body, but had never loved himself, his own body, as he did now. It gave him pleasure to feel the slight pain in his strong leg, to be conscious of the muscles of his chest moving as he breathed. That clear, cool August day which made Anna feel so hopeless seemed exhilarating and invigorating to him...

This is indeed Tolstoy, 'the Seer of the Flesh', who is speaking; and the strange thing is that although Vronsky is showing himself almost indifferent to Anna's own anguish, and her own position, Tolstoy does not seem to blame him for it. He seems to be revelling himself in the idea of love as a stimulus and an addition to that joyful solipsism of the body which is characteristic of so many of his descriptions. Even the style and syntax of this passage, a fact more noticeable in the Russian, although it comes across in translation too, has a kind of detailed awkwardness and literalness which seems to convey the body and its movements. (In terms of style and physical texture Tolstoy can sometimes remind us of D. H. Lawrence: both authors have the same total disregard for that care for, and *niceness* of, style to be found, for example, in Turgenev.)

One of the marvels of *Anna Karenina* as a novel is the way in which a total zest for, and appreciation of, the joys of living merges with but remains unaffected by the ominous signs of misery, loneliness and failure which are visible right from the beginning. The novel opens, after all, with a spectacular failure in a married relation, although it is one that can be and is overcome by a kind of despairing good sense on the woman's part, and a hangdog easygoing good nature on the man's. Stiva Oblonsky and his wife Dolly are very much in the ordinary run of humanity where marriage is concerned, and in terms of structure and psychology they make a perfect foil to Anna and Vronsky: one more subtle and less obvious than the contrasting younger couple, Kitty and Levin.

Many literary critics, including Percy Lubbock in his well-known book *The Art of Fiction*, have criticized Tolstoy for dissipating the effect of his tragic story by intermingling it with the more evidently personal and even autobiographical account of Levin's marriage. Lubbock went so far as to say that novelists with a more rigorous sense of their art – Flaubert, Balzac, or

Henry James – would not have muddled up their subject by such a treatment. The same opinion had already been expressed by the novelist Arnold Bennett. But Tolstoy was of course not interested in the kind of economy of effect preached and practised by these more purist novelists. His idea of the art and its functions was quite different. And whatever view we take of his attitude to the novel (Henry James holding Tolstoy's to be 'a wonderful mass of life', but, in terms of art, no more than 'loose baggy monsters') it must surely be recognized that *Anna Karenina* would be a lesser novel in every way did it not give us the multiple situations and personalities that it does. Its art is indisputable, but it is art on a far wider and more essentially Russian scale than any of the European masters of the form could have achieved.

At this point it is worth noting that Tolstoy himself had drawn a sharp distinction between the kind of writing that he had been attempting in *War and Peace*, and the task that he had set himself in *Anna Karenina*. In the original preface to *War and Peace* he had remarked that 'we Russians do not know how to write novels in the sense in which this genre is understood in Europe', and he went on to say 'What is *War and Peace*? It is not a novel, even less is it a poem, and still less a historical chronicle. *War and Peace* is what the author wished and was able to express in the form in which it is expressed.' This does not get the reader very far, though it shows Tolstoy's typical determination to be tiresomely different. And what he says is also self-evidently true. When he came to write *Anna Karenina*, however, he spoke deliberately of 'this novel, the first I have attempted', and he said, 'I am taking it very seriously'.

What made him consciously think of it as a 'novel', perhaps even in 'the sense in which this genre is understood in Europe'? Two factors contributed perhaps. One was the story itself, the story of a suicide. On the railway quite close to Yasnaya Polyana a woman, the mistress of a local landowner, had thrown herself under a train. As a fellow landowner Tolstoy had to attend the inquiry. The other fact was in a sense a purely technical one, but all the more interesting for that. He had been reading his children some of Pushkin's stories, including one (an unfinished one as it happens) that begins in Pushkin's simple and tersely natural style: 'The guests had just arrived at the *dacha*.' 'That's how to do it', said Tolstoy, 'that's how narrative should go', and he began to make tentative drafts for the start of his own story.

The process was of course nothing like so simple and straightforward as it had appeared to be with Pushkin. The famous opening sentence of *Anna,* which, as an almost playful-sounding epigram, has been compared with that of Jane Austen's *Pride and Prejudice,* only arrived after several beginnings and false starts had been made and discarded. And it seems almost as if we are intended to take it ironically. It is as if the author was saying: well, reader, you are just about to start reading a novel, and to begin with, what about the idea that all happy families resemble one another and all unhappy ones are unhappy in their own separate ways? The second sentence is more incisive. 'Confusion reigned in the house of the Oblonskys.' But this is the kind of confusion that is produced by marital upheavals in every family, while the story of Anna and Vronsky is not so unusual either. Tolstoy must have known this, but he also knew that every complex human situation is indeed quite different from that of any other. It was such knowledge that made him a great novelist, and makes *Anna Karenina* a unique story.

One of the stranger things about the woman herself is how long it took Tolstoy to 'imagine' her. Some heroines – Flaubert's Madame Bovary for example – have clearly come straight, as they are, into their creator's mind and eye. Such was not the case with Anna. In one of the original drafts we meet her early in the story, at a party not unlike that which opens *War and Peace,* and see her, as it were, purely objectively. She is dark, vivacious, and rather stout – 'a little more so,' says her creator ungallantly, 'and she would have appeared monstrous.' As it is she seems just the kind of lively and commonplace woman with a boring husband, who is highly sexed and possibly on the look-out for a lover. How Tolstoy transforms her into the bewitching but also much more physically and mentally mysterious woman of the completed novel is itself something of a mystery. Critics have objected to her lack of 'background' – what was her previous history, and how did she come to marry Karenin? In fact, and it is one of the greatest strengths of the novel, Tolstoy relies here on manipulating the reader's own powers of intuition. As the book gets under way we can *sense* the whole of her, sense even what her childhood and young girlhood must have been like. And – most significantly – her brother is Stiva, that good-natured, selfish, easygoing, amoral man, who has the ability to get out of difficulties, and easily evade or surmount every problem in life.

Anna is a kind of female opposite, or rather converse, of her brother. Where he takes things lightly, she takes them hard. Where he lightly lets feelings and emotions ride, she can be insecure, possessive and passionately jealous. One of the many delightfully comic moments in the novel is Dolly wondering what her husband would do or say if she took a lover, and gloomily conceding to herself, apparently, that he wouldn't notice, and if he did, wouldn't believe it. Above all, the difference between brother and sister is that he is a man, with all the immense advantages of a man of his place, class and epoch, and she is a woman, with all the attendant pitfalls and handicaps that surrounded a woman in her position.

Almost inadvertently therefore, as it would seem, Tolstoy has contributed a powerful demonstration in his novel about the position of women, and the injustice to which society subjects them, indirectly illustrating this with all the life and detail of a great novel. This is what other writers of the nineteenth century like John Stuart Mill had been saying in the form of exposition and polemic. Anna is a victim, like all women in her position. But of course she is highly individualized: all unhappy women are unhappy in their own way. And as her story unfolds the question in it seems to be asked with increasing insistence: what social change is necessary to end this kind of suffering, to make it possible for men and women to live freely together in society, to follow the road of their own passions and desires and live in the way that best suits them?

Did Tolstoy mean to ask this question? He was deeply interested, in his usual didactic often overbearing way, in what was already becoming known as 'the Woman Question' and particularly in the freedom of wives to divorce. At the time he held strong views on the family, and on the right and need of some women, who might reject the idea of children and husband, being able to lead their own independent lives and do good in society in other ways. But he was also a Russian aristocrat, and a paternalist at heart. He expects women to be 'womanly' in the sense that they should run a home and have a natural authority in it, under the man. In this sense Anna is not womanly; and with his usual remorseless perspicacity Tolstoy shows us Anna's natural inability to run things and to be a conventional wife. No doubt it is something in her family background; and once again the figure of her brother Stiva enters the picture, feckless, dreaming of girls with breasts like champagne glasses, and naturally expecting everything to be done for him, whether at home or elsewhere. And of course so it is; but for Anna it is not; and, quite apart from Vronsky later on, she finds herself at the beginning of life – warm, hopeful, impulsive and ready to please as she had been – thrust into a match with a rather dull but perfectly presentable man, who seems destined for the highest office. It seemed a good idea, and she took it on with all the insouciance that her brother might have had. In fact he was no doubt one of those who encouraged it.

And so there is Anna, as her sister-in-law Dolly has long since noticed, not really belonging in her own home, and making rather too much of her role as mother, even though she does passionately and naturally love her son, and will love him all the more when she is threatened with being deprived of him. Tolstoy is pitiless in revealing what to him is radically at fault, even though he never draws the reader's attention to it but lets it emerge gradually through the narrative. It is Dolly again who spots that Anna behaves like a guest in her own house, even after – or rather, especially after – she has gone off with Vronsky, and is living at his opulent country estate. It is Vronsky who runs everything there, giving a considering glance round the dinner-table, catching the butler's eye. We remember finding out earlier in the story that Vronsky has never known family life, having been an only son, with a selfish, worldly and possessive mother. Now he is self-consciously and rather pathetically playing at being the head of a family, with no wife to embody for him how it naturally and simply happens.

It is these details that go to the heart of Tolstoy's process, and are the secret of his extraordinary authority as a novelist. He deploys them as minutely and copiously as he had done in *War and Peace*; but in *Anna Karenina* they have a deeply domestic, almost claustrophobic density, even though they are continually lit up by flashes of comedy, and of comic relief. The reader is also conscious that Tolstoy is not so thoroughly at ease with himself as he was in the previous work, and that he is conscious all the time of where the story is leading, and what conclusions must be drawn from it. Where *War and Peace* breaks off, as if everything and everybody in it are healthily tired and going to bed and to sleep, to awake refreshed in a new morning, *Anna Karenina* makes towards a destined ending which is at once tragic and anticlimactic. Anna dies her solitary death, almost like a rat in a corner, half forgotten by the other characters. (One of the book's most poignant moments is her call on Dolly and Kitty near the end, who remark to each other after she leaves that something unusual seems to be the matter with her, but are too preoccupied with their own affairs to take it in.) And in the painful coda after her death Vronsky is seen setting out for the Balkan war, which is meaningless to him, but may offer some distraction. And he can think of nothing but an appalling toothache which has suddenly come on.

At some point in the composition of his novel, Tolstoy added the epigraph from the Bible that stands at its head – 'Vengeance is mine: I will repay.' His motive in doing so is obscure, and possibly shows a real uncertainty – something very rare in his forceful and opinionated nature – about what he wanted the novel to be and to say. It may even have been a gesture towards public feeling or prejudice; Anna was a sinner who should not be judged by men, but would discover the justice of God? But Tolstoy had no belief in a biblical God of either the Old or the New Testament; nor did he necessarily feel that Anna would or should suffer punishment in the world's eye, or in God's.

In his early drafts for the novel we can see him trying out all sorts of possible solutions and conclusions – ways in which the novel might end, or ought to end. None of them seemed right. In one tentative early version the couple marry after Anna's divorce, and have two children. Both Anna and Vronsky are more commonplace than they are in the final story, and get along pretty well after their earlier passion has subsided, although Vronsky begins to regret more and more his abandoned career, and Anna her lost social status. Indeed this version does contain explicitly what in the novel, as it was finished, is never stated openly, although like so much else in the rich complex pattern it remains importantly undefined. This is the tyranny that any society can exercise almost unconsciously over its members, however much they may ignore it, or seek to defy it. Anna and Vronsky are not in fact the free agents that they felt they would become when they have their way, and break away.

Why is this? The question remains an important one, even today, when social emancipation seems complete, and the social acceptance of divorce, remarriage, or living together without benefit of either, is taken totally for granted. None the less many women even today may find themselves in something like Anna's situation, when she goes to the theatre after the whole scandal has long subsided, and is still ignored by all her former friends and grand acquaintances. Of course any social setting today would be quite different, but it may still exercise pressures on the individual of which he or she may hardly be aware until the crunch comes. Tolstoy has a horribly expert intuition where things of this sort are concerned, just as he does in an even more painful area: the fact that Anna – inexplicably to herself and others – cannot love the little daughter she has by Vronsky as she loves her son by Karenin, Seryozha. It is as if her maternal instinct, and its natural immediacy, has been burnt or bled out in some way, not only by the force of her new passion but by the suffering and deprivation that it has entailed.

For Anna feels no guilt as such: that is one of the masterstrokes of Tolstoy's intuition. For Karenin and her past life she feels no more than might a shipwrecked sailor in a lifeboat for those who have been left to drown. She feels only for her lost son, like an animal deprived of its young. Nor is it guilt or sorrow in any conventional sense that oppresses her as time goes on, but an equally primitive and spontaneous though to her new and unfamiliar emotion – sexual jealousy. There is nothing Dickensian or Victorian about Anna's eventual suicide, none of the proper feelings of remorse or expiation. She does it as most suicides do – perhaps the one also near Yasnaya Polyana that prompted Tolstoy to begin the novel – in a momentary fit almost of pique, of 'I'll show him'. Poor Anna. And almost the last thing she notices, as the carriage drives to the station, is a hairdresser's shop with a comic name. I'll tell that to him she thinks – for sharing a joke together is one of the truest pleasures and intimacies of a marriage – and then she remembers that she won't be seeing him again.

Poor Anna! And the way the reader feels this is indeed Tolstoy's triumph. The reader is passionately sorry for Anna. But all the Annas of the earlier drafts are characterless, because seen in some way too objectively. The final Anna is completely individualized, and yet is equally clearly very much a part of Tolstoy himself. 'Madame Bovary, c'est moi', remarked her creator Flaubert. Tolstoy could have said the same of Anna, although one can't imagine him doing it – indeed he would have been much annoyed at the suggestion. But there is no doubt that Tolstoy's feeling for Anna's situation is a very intimate one, however secret; and that it was because he himself had come increasingly to feel exiled from the life he had chosen, or that had chosen him. While writing *Anna Karenina* he often longed to get away from home, and even to become one of the mad holy men who wandered the distances of Russia, and whose appearance at Yasnaya Polyana when he was 7 or 8 he had recorded so memorably in *Childhood*. What physical passion and life with Vronsky was in its appeal to Anna, so the freedom of a tramp and an outcast must have seemed at the time to Tolstoy. It is hardly too much to say that the book is the record of a great change in his life; and, even more importantly, the reason why he never wrote anything again of the same kind. He, the man who understood individuals and classes and social life so deeply and intuitively, would give all that up and turn to matters of the spirit and the ideal life, to the problem of how men should live, and what they should live by. The writer's task was finished and the teacher's had begun. Was it a sacrifice? – almost like Anna's giving up her son?

What is certain is that Tolstoy could not be happy any more as the Rostovs had been happy, as Anna and Vronsky expected to be happy in their new life together, and found too late that they could not be. There is something strangely moving but also gruesome in the last quarter of the novel, when the lovers are pretending that they have everything they want, and that all is well. One of the most interesting commentaries on the novel is that by D. H. Lawrence, who maintained in one of his casual but vivid essays, also in letters and in a doggerel rhyme, that Tolstoy had been afraid to face the consequences of his own invention of Anna and Vronsky – the essentially *liberated* pair – whose example, and whose bravery in cocking a snook at society, should have been an example to Russia and to the world.

Lawrence was of course thinking of his own example, and of his own elopement with Frieda, the German aristocrat. That had worked – why should not the Russian pair have found the same realization? But Lawrence of course ignores the fact that he and

Frieda were, quite simply, *not* the pair of individuals that Tolstoy had created in Anna and Vronsky. Lawrence could do his work anywhere: Frieda was a *gamine* and a bohemian by nature. Lawrence preferred to ignore the uniqueness of an individual, and the mysterious question of what 'his life means to him', as Tolstoy had put it in *War and Peace*.

For Lawrence it was not a question of what the woman was like but what the woman *was* – and that was something he was sure that he – and he alone – knew best. And the same for the man? Oddly enough, Tolstoy and Lawrence share in many ways exactly the same kind of dogmatism and 'he knew he was rightness', as it might be called. But Lawrence was less of a divided man, or a divided genius. His whole message, in fact, is of unity and wholeness, in being either man or woman. Perhaps because he belongs to his age, as well as in virtue of his background and temperament, Tolstoy remained always internally tormented and unsure, always a thwarted and at times an all but hopeless seeker, striving to obtain something that was not in his own individual nature.

His greatest works are in a sense, and paradoxically, a relief from his intellectual self and his yearnings, a turning to what came most naturally to him, and most offered a kind of relaxation. He wrote his great novels, one could almost say without being frivolous, under the same impulse that led him to enquire of his daughter what the girls and young men were wearing at the St Petersburg balls. F. R. Leavis, a shrewd critic who sometimes compared Tolstoy unfavourably with Lawrence, remarked that he was too easily seduced as a writer of fiction by anything that savoured of the *beau monde*. That verdict makes the same point. And what is certainly true is that Tolstoy himself repudiated his own best and greatest work, and came to feel that his major novels were worthless.

4

Stories and Theories

It remains to consider the reasons for Tolstoy's own verdict, and what were the consequences for his own writing. If Tolstoy was a fox who longed passionately to be a hedgehog – to refer back to Isaiah Berlin's distinction – he would of course in time come to reject everything that made him a fox, everything that is most literary and most artful in his novels – most fox-like in fact.

And this is indeed what happened. Before he had completed *A Confession*, inspired as it was by the horror of what he called the Arzamas experience, he had begun other investigations into religious belief, and what he now felt about it. The result was 'A Criticism of Dogmatic Theology', and the full-length book *What I Believe*, both of them fairly unreadable for most people today. The very simplicity and forcefulness of these works seems to militate against them; for Tolstoy, having assured himself that he and he alone has suddenly seen what should be obvious to all, proceeds to reiterate it, while holding the reader like an ancient mariner with his glittering eye. From Christ's teaching he accepts five commandments. No anger, no oath-swearing, no adultery; do not defend yourself; do not go to war. (More controversial aspects of Christ's teaching, such as 'I came not to bring peace on earth but a sword', which so much perplexed and upset Levin in *Anna Karenina*, can presumably be discarded.)

These teachings, he tells us are incontrovertibly laid down by Christ. They refer religion to daily life, and they are the foundation of all Tolstoy's subsequent beliefs, particularly pacifism and non-violence. In them he had found the answer to what had seemed the insuperably stubborn question: 'What gives meaning to a man's life?' for he writes that 'there is a power enabling me to discern what is good. My reason and conscience proceed from it and the purpose of conscious life can only be to do its will – that is, to do good.'

That the acutely sceptical and analytical Tolstoy should find new and absolute meaning for himself in this is perhaps not so surprising as the fact that he could abandon so completely what must be called the worldly common sense that underlies his view of life in the novels. Tolstoy's progress can be seen psychologically as a process of going backward: back to something that often resembles the callow dogmatism and arrogance of his youth. He has become again the only man in step; the man, too, who has given up his close and careful observation of mankind, as if that were in itself inimical to the discovery of truth. He had become terrified by the voice of scepticism in any form. And yet at the same time the power of his intellect remained quite undiminished, and he was able to deploy his knowledge of Greek and Hebrew, as well as a whole library of biblical commentators, in order to probe the difficulties of interpretation of the gospels. The Holy Synod of the Orthodox church were alarmed enough by his new knowledge to take what he said very seriously indeed, and in their official journal, the *Church Gazette*, they formally excluded him from the Russian church, though with the provision that he would be admitted back if he renounced his heresies.

In 1881 Tsar Alexander II was assassinated by a group of terrorists, and Tolstoy at once wrote an impassioned but respectful letter to the new Tsar, in which he pleaded for the lives of the murderers, who had been apprehended. It says much for the power and influence that Tolstoy had begun to exercise over hearts and minds in Russia, even in court circles, that Alexander III received his appeal with courteous seriousness (what would Stalin have done?) and caused a reply to be sent, though its authenticity remains uncertain. In it he said that if it were himself, and he had survived, he would have been prepared to pardon an attempt on his own life, but he could not take upon himself the right to pardon the murderers of his father. This eminently reasonable reply contrasts with the unworldly fervour with which Tolstoy himself had addressed the Tsar. 'One word of forgiveness and Christian love, spoken and fulfilled from the height of the throne, and the path of Christian rule which is before you, waiting to be trod, can destroy the evil that is corroding Russia... Every revolutionary struggle will melt away before the man-Tsar who fulfils the law of Christ.'

The murderers were not pardoned, and it would have made not the slightest difference to the revolutionaries and their aims if they had been. Dostoevsky saw that with penetrating clarity, and in his novel *The Devils* he described their aims with far greater accuracy and insight than the now unworldly Tolstoy could have done. Like many of those who have suddenly seen the light, Tolstoy seemed wilfully determined to fly in the face of all the sense and knowledge of things that he had once so abundantly possessed. That knowledge can be summed up in a comment he made at the time he was writing *Anna Karenina*, and which probably referred especially to his difficulties with the character of Anna herself. 'It is a bad thing for an artist', he said, 'when a character is forced by him to do what is not in their nature.' So, in the unwinding of the plot of his second and last great novel, he had not forced the heroine to behave unnaturally, or to go outside the limits of her true being. He had understood and allowed for the full complexity of her situation, and had found, as he put it, that no matter what he did Anna always ended up under a train at the railway station. The reader sees exactly why, and in terms of Anna's life, her situation and limitations, can only agree with the verdict.

But now the Tolstoy who would write in *What is Art?* that social effectiveness was the sole criterion of artistic success had begun compelling not only his characters but people in general, and even his own family, to act in ways that were contrary to their natures. Powerful and learned as they are, his polemical works, to which he now added the tract *What Then Must We Do?*, can hardly persuade anyone who is not already persuaded and prepared to become what from now on had begun to be called a Tolstoyan. Not that Tolstoy's artistic work ever really ceased, however ambivalent his view of it had become. In 1886 he produced two powerful stories, 'The Devil' and *The Death of Ivan Ilyich*, the first a study in sexual obsession and jealousy, inspired by the guilt and disgust he felt about his own love affairs on the estate; and the second an even more compelling account of an ordinary man, a civil servant, who falls ill, gets worse, and finally dies.

What we notice about both tales, masterly as they are, is the author's determination to make them function as he wills, and produce the moral effect that he wants. Action and outcome are preconceived, and the purpose of the writer is paramount. Prince

Mirsky, Tolstoy's shrewdest but most sympathetic commentator, wrote that before 1880 Tolstoy saw life as an enchanted ballroom: after that date as the black bag into which the dying Ivan Ilyich feels himself inexorably pushed at the end of the story. Moreover, Tolstoy is determined not only that the poor man should experience death in this hideously claustrophobic fashion, but that at the last moment he should be released into a sense of freedom and light. As Tolstoy had himself obviously experienced neither of these states that he wished upon his character, the ending of *The Death of Ivan Ilyich* is the supreme example of his conviction that he now knew best about everything, on *a priori* grounds. In his earlier work, by contrast, we feel that he never writes about or analyses anything that he has not experienced himself, and in consequence is able to make his readers feel that they have experienced it too.

But this is by no means the case, or the feeling the reader has, with *Master and Man*, the powerful tale that Tolstoy wrote nearly ten years later. In the meanwhile he had written a large number of cautionary tales, as they might not unfairly be called, many of which, like 'What Men Live By' were addressed to children. With his usual shrewdness Tolstoy remarked that 'one should write for the young as one did for grown-ups, only better'. Children were harder to take in. 'What Men Live By', like all the best tales of this time, is beautifully crafted and not too insistent on its moral, although there is no doubt of its being there. God sends an angel down to earth to live by love, but things do not go quite according to plan. In 'How Much Land Does a Man Need?' a greedy peasant (and all peasants were greedy and grasping about land, as Tolstoy well knew) finds out too late that the only land he really needs is the six foot in which he is buried. One of the most genuinely amusing tales is 'The Imp and the Crust', in which the devil tempts a kindly peasant into becoming a drunkard. The message about learning to lay off the vodka, never an untimely one in Russia, is never explicitly stated, but remains a conclusion readers must draw for themselves, not that they would have much trouble in doing so. But Tolstoy came increasingly to feel, and no doubt rightly, that the simpler his readers the harder they were to take in. Their natural suspicions would only be aroused if they saw too clearly what the writer intended them to see.

Tolstoy was encouraged to write these tales by his in many

ways sinister disciple Chertkov, the ex-Guards officer who obtained so much influence over him in the last period of his life. Chertkov wanted the great writer to make money 'for the cause', and he certainly succeeded in this aim, for the books that Tolstoy chose or wrote himself – they went by the name of 'Intermediary Books' and were sold at a cheap price by a Moscow publisher – were printed and sold in millions during the eighties and nineties. It was of course a period when the propaganda story, written for the sake of a number of causes, was in vogue all round the world, and widely in demand through the increasing spread of elementary education. (It is an odd fact that Henry James's first short story had been written for a temperance magazine and is equally adroit, compared to Tolstoy's, at putting in the obligatory moral without drawing attention to it.)

Master and Man, one of the best tales Tolstoy ever wrote, is a rather different matter. There is no moral, or rather the moral is a highly ambiguous one; and to that extent we are back in the world of *War and Peace* and *Anna Karenina*, where, as Shestov observed, nothing is as straightforward as it seems, and where even the style, simple and forceful as it always is, is none the less hedged about with continual subtleties, additions and qualifications. In the later stories, intended to reach peasants and children, Tolstoy produces a much more deliberate simplicity – spare, functional and beautifully effective, but far more self-conscious than the earlier manner. In *Master and Man*, as in the novella *Hadji Murad*, which Tolstoy wrote about the Caucasus in the last decade of his life, the manner is still extremely simple, but almost enigmatically so. We feel, as when reading Kleist, or Kafka, that all self-consciousness and intention have been peeled away.

In *Master and Man* the rich peasant Brekhunov sets out by sled on a winter journey to do a deal. Night comes on; there is a violent blizzard, and he and his driver lose their way. Nothing for it but to wrap up as well as they can and wait till morning. Brekhunov has a fur coat and wraps, but his driver is ill-clad and is soon shivering. Two things occur to the master at the same moment. His driver will die of cold if left as he is, and he himself may die of cold if he doesn't help to keep his driver warm. The reflection makes him feel happy, and they huddle together as best they can. In the morning Brekhunov is dead, frozen, and the hardier driver is barely alive: nor is he particularly grateful when, after being rescued, he finds his hands and feet are frostbitten, and may never be of much use again. Death for the master comes without either terror or meaning, and the story ends without comment, and without the metaphor with which the author emphasized his ending in *The Death of Ivan Ilyich*.

5

Hadji Murad and the Plays

With *Hadji Murad* Tolstoy does indeed clamp his tale within the vice of a metaphor, just as he had done with the black bag in *Ivan Ilyich*. And yet the metaphor in this case has no significance outside itself: it makes the wonderfully told story virtually seem like a parable without a point. This effect makes it one of the most striking things that Tolstoy ever wrote. The metaphor is the tough and sturdy thistle, called by the peasants a 'Tartar' thistle, which resists being grubbed up from a cultivated field. At the beginning and ending of the story Tolstoy compares it to the indomitable old native Tartar chieftain, Hadji Murad of the Caucasus, about whom he had heard many years before, when he was there in the army as a young man.

Hadji Murad had long been a thorn in the side of the occupying Russian power. At length he had decided to co-operate, and had come to confer with the Russian commandant; for some reason he began to suspect trickery, and he determined to escape from his Cossack escort and go back to a rebel life in the mountains. He is pursued, overtaken and killed, and that is the end of the story. From its nature and background the story could be romantic, in the manner of Sir Walter Scott or his numerous Russian imitators who wrote epic tales about the Caucasus. In fact Tolstoy makes the story a complex narrative demonstration – its air of transparent simplicity is deceptive – in which the participation of the reader is not solicited in any way, as it is in his other 'simple' stories. Here we are to see, but not to share; and not to draw conclusions. So far from being a romantic dream like Scott, or a didactic tale like the Tolstoyan tales that preceded it, it is more like Shakespeare. This is because of the manner in which it unfolds inside its metaphorical setting, bringing in the widest implications – for instance that of imperial power – but making no explicit commentary or judgement.

It was the work of Tolstoy's most admired by the philosopher Wittgenstein – he was also very impressed by 'God Sees the Truth but Waits' – who praised its extreme clarity and objectivity. However full of admiration, that verdict is perhaps none the less somewhat misleading; for when looked into closely this masterful tale reveals itself to be as full of Tolstoyan tendentiousness as any of his other work, although purpose is presented here with great cunning and with a complete absence of that air of always 'knowing best' which used to distinguish the writer's manner previously. The discipline of writing tracts and cautionary tales has given the older Tolstoy the cunning of a preacher who has now learnt how essential it is to appear before his audience in all humility, and to conceal his authority from them.

The tale has one significant point in common with *The Cossacks*. Both stress, though with a different emphasis in each case, the futility of human endeavour. In his later years Tolstoy was always preaching that the certain road to disappointment and failure for anyone was to try to get what they wanted; and these stories demonstrate this truth in their own oblique and graphic fashion. *The Cossacks* ends with the failure of the young Olenin's conceited and self-satisfied attempts to understand and to join in the Cossack way of life. In his much more mature and dignified way Hadji Murad has attempted, for the sake of himself and his people, to respond to Russian offers and throw in his lot with them, to be on the winning side. That too ends in failure, and in his own death. It would not be going too far to say that both of these long and in their different ways compelling novellas have an inner meaning, which concerned the author himself. They suggest a hidden awareness – both when the author was young and when he was old – that everything he did and sought after – sought indeed to dominate and to control – was bound to end the same way. Tolstoy's confidence in being always right was never that of a self-deceiver.

More rewarding, however, is to study the inconspicuous narrative method Tolstoy adopts in this greatest of all his tales. He extends to its limit the 'scenic' method he used in more casual and diluted form in his long novels; and here it becomes a method which may remind the reader still more of the swift alternation and contrast of scenes in Shakespearean drama (which is ironical in view of Tolstoy's expressed dislike of Shakespeare in *What is Art?*). The sequence is highly scenic rather than chronological. After meeting Hadji Murad we leave him abruptly to meet in the Russian fort the young commandant Vorontsov and his wife, switching back to the Tartar camp where Hadji Murad is still considering how best to approach the Russians. Then the peepshow abruptly moves to Russia, and to the Tsar at his capital, St Petersburg. On the day the Russian soldier Avdeev is mortally wounded in the Caucasus we are with his family in Russia, where his father is threshing rye with the soldier's brother, in whose place he was sent off to join the army. He has not been back since, 'for in those days the conscription was like death'. The quiet weight of that comment is like the blows of the flail on the threshing floor, heavy and unhurried; and the reader here can see exactly how this process was carried out. It is *War and Peace* on a miniature but even more detailed scale.

When the news of her son's death arrives, together with the rouble note she had sent him, the old farmer's wife 'weeps for as long as she can spare time'; and the soldier's wife is secretly glad. Now she can make the shopman, with whom she had been secretly living, marry her.

Unhurriedly the scenes alternate and continue; and in the most brilliant time shift of all we are shown the hero's severed head before we are given the climactic set-piece of his last battle.

> It was a shaven head with salient brows, short black beard and moustache, one eye open and the other half-closed. The shaven skull was cleft, but not right through, and there was congealed blood at the nose. The blue lips still bore a kindly childlike expression.

The woman who is living with the commandant of the fort, to which the dead hero's head is brought, turns away in disgust, saying like the epic heroine Antigone that a dead body should be given back to the earth. The officer shrugs his shoulders, saying 'That's war', and that it might have happened to himself.

Considering that Tolstoy professed to dislike Shakespeare and to consider him overvalued, as he tells us in an exaggerated and even perverse way in 'What is Art?', there is a certain irony in the fact that Shakespeare's presence is so manifold in the background of his finest story. But that is the kind of paradox that goes with the instinctive genius great artists possess. The deepest inspiration is seldom or never admitted openly, as Tolstoy had generously admitted the presiding influence of *David Copperfield* in the composition and *Childhood* and *Boyhood*. Nor does he now admit that even as he was depreciating the fashionable young French writer Guy de Maupassant in one of his most forceful critical essays, he was probably inclined himself to write his last stories in a manner that was not so distant from that of the new French writer – brief and impersonal, economical and impassive – especially when describing graphic sequences and moments. The 'wordy' tendencies and the proliferating qualifications and subordinate clauses have been pared away, and Tolstoy's naturally luxuriant Russian syntax has become spare, and almost Gallic.

Moreover, if there is something Shakespearean about *Hadji Murad* it may be not unconnected with the fact that Tolstoy in his last period himself took to writing plays. One of them, *The Live Corpse*, he himself thought his best; and he remarked that it and *Hadji Murad* were the only two of his latterday works he really valued. ('Yes, the old man wrote it well', he commented dryly when one of his friends praised the story, and wished he would write more like it.) Both story and play have much in common. Both achieve a new and dramatic relation between author and protagonist, and both substitute a technique of dramatic exchange for the usual Tolstoyan assertion. In one sense play and story even seem more and not less autobiographical than the big novels, for in them we detect the hidden hand of Tolstoy instead of merely seeing him plain, as we see him in the Levin of *Anna Karenina*. Just as it might be said that the real Tolstoy of *Anna Karenina* was the heroine herself, trapped in a society and a situation that becomes increasingly false for her, so in the later play and story we have heroes who strive to escape from an impossible situation, and fail. In *Hadji Murad* and *The Live Corpse* Tolstoy cut off all overt connection with himself, and assumed a wholly impartial air, but this makes the underlying identification even more intense.

Fedya, the 'live corpse' of the play has pretended to commit suicide, in order to free his wife, and the virtuous and upright man who loves her, from the burden of his own shiftless and inconvenient existence. In relation to the Countess Tolstoy the irony may be obvious to us, though it does not seem to have occurred to anyone at the time. Tolstoy's new style and dramatic technique covered his tracks well. When Fedya's deception is revealed in the latter part of the play, his wife and her by now new husband are charged with bigamy, and Fedya only saves the situation by committing suicide in earnest. In another sense, as it might be said, there was no way for Tolstoy himself to abandon the world he inhabited by nature as aristocrat and landowner, family man and member of high society, except to remove himself from it by flight or death. Otherwise he would go on being a nuisance to everybody, and to his wife a cross she found increasingly hard to bear. For Hadji Murad the dilemma was not so dissimilar. He too tried to abandon his way of life, and was trusted neither by the Russians nor by his own people. He remembers the tale of the falcon, who was caught by men, and then pecked to death by its own kind when it escaped back into the wild.

If Tolstoy had written nothing but plays he would probably hardly have been heard of, and been now quite forgotten; and yet his plays are by no means without point or power, even though they are obviously the work of an author with little love for the theatre, or understanding of its peculiar effects and artifices. While working on *War and Peace* he had dashed off a five-act farce, *The Contaminated Family,* a satire on the sort of people who join radical movements, and live off society while denouncing all its ways. It is significant that Tolstoy was in his own way celebrating old Russian ways and customs in his great work of the time, and *The Contaminated Family* – significant title – was very much the opposite of the true and real Russian families who support the world of *War and Peace.* One wonders what would have been his reaction to Orwell's comment about England being a family with the wrong members in charge. That was not so far from being the view of the young radicals in Russia in the 1860s, and Tolstoy was certainly going against the intellectual spirit of that decade. It is perhaps hardly surprising that his at first eager attempts to have the play produced came to nothing, and he never tried to publish it.

The Nihilist, written two years later, was a light-hearted comedy intended to be acted at home; and after that Tolstoy attempted nothing more for the theatre until 1886, when he dramatized his own short story about drunkenness, 'The Imp and the Crust', and also produced what became his most celebrated play *The Power of Darkness.* Famous as it became, it is also curiously wooden and inept in terms of dramatic effect, full of monologues and self-denunciations. Bernard Shaw admired it, and while shrewd about its shortcomings singled out for special praise a scene in which the old soldier tries to persuade the young criminal protagonist to confess. The strongest feature in the play is the rivalry between the young man's wife and her stepdaughter, his mistress; but the murder of the stepdaughter's illegitimate child, and the melodrama of the confession, seem artificial and Dostoevskian, out of key with the author's natural bent, even though it is clear that he has a complete understanding of the sort of grim peasant life which he presents.

When the play was finally put on in St Petersburg in 1895, the event was hailed as a victory against the censorship, and Tolstoy found himself lionized by the sort of young radicals he had satirized in *The Contaminated Family.* His own family had its triumph a few years earlier, when some of his children discovered the draft of a comedy he had written some time before and put aside, and persuaded him to put it on for them at home at Yasnaya Polyana. He was reluctant at first, maintaining that the theatre was an amusement for the idle rich, but eventually he entered into the spirit of the thing, and *The Fruits of Enlightenment* as he now called it was a tremendous popular and local success. It also became Tolstoy's most widely known and successful play from its first production by the young Stanislavsky, then just starting out on his career, and it has always maintained its stage popularity. Rightly, because the satire on the gentry is effective but fair, and the idea of an extended Russian family, in which classes both combine together and intrigue against each other, is done with a humour and kindness rare in Tolstoy's later work. Harmony is unforced, and comedy sharp without being sour.

6

Last Stories and *Resurrection*

In the dozen or so years between the late eighties and the late nineties Tolstoy produced three works of fiction. The first, *The Kreutzer Sonata*, is in many ways odd and perverse, but it is the most revelatory of all the author's works about his attitudes to his own sex life. Like many other novelists, Tolstoy was fond of taking some aspect of himself and exaggerating it in the presentation of a character. Thus Olenin in *The Cossacks* represented the young Tolstoy's callow self-conceit, and conviction that he understands things and people; Pierre in *War and Peace*, an exaggeratedly Tolstoyan fumbling and uncertain, though passionate, search for the truth. Pozdnyshev in *The Kreutzer Sonata* is a kind of malignant and self-hating doll who reveals a hatred of sex and an obsession with it which goes far beyond anything his creator ever expressed in person.

The story is effectively structured. Its narrator meets an odd man in a train and hears his story, and his theories about life and sex, which are striking and absorbing in their very contradictoriness. Pozdnyshev has murdered his wife, out of jealousy as he says, although the 'I' of the story gradually begins to feel it was really out of hatred and exasperation with the whole idea and world of marriage itself. Jealousy was caused by the wife's infatuation with a musician friend, the pair often playing Beethoven's Kreutzer Sonata together. Tolstoy, who thought all music had highly physical effects, felt that the Sonata stirred sex feelings almost as strong as the music of *Don Giovanni*, which he held should never be played when the two sexes were in close proximity under a roof. This kind of susceptibility drives Pozdnyshev into a state of obsessive fantasy, and he finally stabs his wife with an ornamental dagger which is hanging on the wall. The act of murder itself is a remarkable example of Tolstoyan detailed realism. The wife's corset resists the blow, and in the act of striking the blow the murderer notices that the dagger sheath drops behind a sofa. 'I must remember that or it will get lost.' The wife survives, but dies later from the wound she has received.

Tolstoy wrote to a friend as he produced successive drafts of the story that the idea in it was beginning 'to take hold of him', and that he was becoming convinced that married chastity was not only an ideal but a duty. At first, he said, 'I became horrified at the idea', but then he started to accept it as a part of his new outlook and philosophy. He suggested to his wife that they should sleep apart, which shocked her deeply after their twenty-seven years of married life together, and indeed their marriage never really recovered from the effects of *The Kreutzer Sonata*, and the baleful notoriety it achieved. The church attacked Tolstoy and the press behaved odiously, hinting both that the grapes must now be sour for the once revered novelist of love and high society, and also that he was a hypocrite. It was indeed true that his wife had born their thirteenth and last child during the year he began the story; and it was also true that he had told his biographer Aylmer Maude that he still made love to his wife, but that 'I must not abandon the struggle. God grant that I may not do so again.' With the same perversity that the hero of his story was displaying, he also wrote to his disciple Chertkov, whom he had urged to marry for the sake of his health and to procreate, that his doctrines were now reversed. Chastity inside marriage must be the ideal.

The involuntary absurdity, the pathos and the tragicomedy in the business, gets into the story itself and has given to it its curiously unsettling and at the same time slightly ludicrous quality... Tolstoy would once have been aware of this: perhaps he could be so no longer? When the 'I' of the story objects that if Pozdnyshev's ideas were really practised life would disappear, he replies: 'But why live? If life has no aim, if life is given us for life's sake, there is no reason for living.' The whole world of *War and Peace* contradicts that view, but all such things were behind Tolstoy now, and there is no doubt he sometimes felt the despair and revulsion of his hero in *The Kreutzer Sonata*, and the corresponding need to force the meaning of life somehow to reveal itself.

At the same time his old literary sense and skills had not deserted him. He cunningly makes it the 'thought' of his hero, which he 'prized very highly' that 'life for life's sake is not worth living'. This is going behind the character's back, as it were, and not the 'self-derision genuinely Russian' which had made the puzzled Pierre so engaging a character, and his relation to his creator so successful and so much in harmony. Tolstoy does to Pozdnyshev what he had also done to Ivan Ilyich, and what in some degree we would do to Prince Nekhlyudov in *Resurrection*: force them to present his ideas and obsessions without having a true character of their own. It makes us remember again his earlier comment about Anna Karenina: that it was a bad thing when a writer made his characters act and behave in a way that was not in their nature.

Tolstoy presents marriage more directly and more searchingly than any other writer. In *Family Happiness* he theorizes about it; in *War and Peace* and *Anna Karenina* he describes it; in *The Kreutzer Sonata* he denounces it. In a sense they all present the same marriage, but the viewpoint is different. Andrew and his 'Little Princess', Pierre and Hélène, Pierre and Natasha, Anna and Karenin, Anna and Vronsky: they have all undergone the same states of delight and wonderment, disillusion, depression, rage, disgust, acquiescence: but these marriages did not stay in the same state all the time, or indeed for very long. They were in constant flux and movement. The life unfolding in the novel carried them along, dissipating successive impressions and creating new ones, returning them to the first state without consciousness of repetition. As in 'The Devil' and in *The Death of Ivan Ilyich, The Kreutzer Sonata* presents not a living state but a purely hypothetical one. Like many more ordinary stories, they indulge both in nightmare and in daydream.

> I think of running away from her, hiding myself, going to America. I get as far as thinking how I shall get rid of her, how splendid that will be, and I shall unite myself with another, an admirable woman – quite different...

So thinks Pozdnyshev. So many married persons have thought, including Tolstoy himself no doubt, but the thought does not usually persist for long. Other things intervene, and life goes on, as it does in the big novels. But in these stories a particular section of experience is isolated by Tolstoy, as if in a test-tube, and made to represent the whole of living.

The same air of a hypothesis presides over *Resurrection*, which he began in 1890 or a little earlier, but which was not published until the century was nearly ended. It might not have been finished at all had it not been for the stimulus afforded by the case of the Dukhobors, a pacifist farming sect who had been much persecuted by the government, and who were now offered the chance of migrating to Canada. Tolstoy offered to help finance this emigration by the sale of *Resurrection*, an arrangement which greatly annoyed his wife, but which produced one of his old bursts of creative energy.

At the same time, *Resurrection* suffers from the need its author felt to write in accordance with the didactic views on art he had expressed in his theoretical essays; and it is this didacticism which finally triumphs and kills off the old harmonies and ambiguities which give so much density of 'felt life' (in Henry James's phrase) to the two longer novels. Like 'God Sees the Truth but Waits' and 'How Much Land Does a Man Need?', *Resurrection* is essentially one of the cautionary tales, although one of far greater length. In his numerous drafts and reworkings, even more numerous than those of *Anna Karenina*, one can see the difficulty Tolstoy has in reconciling his new ideas about artistic purpose with his old instincts and genius for the novel form.

Not unlike that of Anna, the story itself is based on something he had heard from an acquaintance, a lawyer. One of his clients had seduced a girl and then found himself on the jury at her trial for stealing, as a prostitute. After her conviction he obtained permission to marry her, but she fell ill and died soon after release. This was the story which for purposes of preaching a good moral, and of awakening his readers' consciences, Tolstoy stuck to closely, whereas the equally simple beginnings of *Anna Karenina* had led him into all sorts of complex observations and side-issues. It is probably true, too, that Tolstoy was especially stirred by personal guilt feelings in the case of *Resurrection*. The lawyer's story reminded him of at least one not so dissimilar moment in his own career, when he had seduced a maid who subsequently came to grief. So he told his biographer, though his wife maintained that he in fact exaggerated the bad consequences of his act.

However that may be, the girl Maslova and her seducer Prince Nekhlyudov remain through the novel just the kind of people who would suit the outlines of a cautionary tale. They do not have any character other than that the story requires, but within these limits their presentation is very successful, as is that of the many minor characters, particularly those the prince meets on his journey to Siberia in the attempt to rescue Maslova. As it happens we have, in one sense, met the prince before, in the narrative of *Boyhood* and *Youth*. There he was the friend of the narrator Irtenyev, who sees and describes him with that almost involuntarily exact and sharp eye the young Tolstoy so abundantly possessed, and used. Briefly analysing Nekhlyudov, the narrator says that he couldn't exercise the faculty of *understanding* which most persons in a family possess (and which he possesses himself of course). In this crucial respect Nekhlyudov's undoubted intelligence becomes rather obtuse. For example, says Irtenyev, he is the kind of man who takes things like honour and morals, religion or patriotism, seriously, whereas true 'understanders' see through them or round them, always understanding just 'where empty phrases begin'.

It is impossible to know whether Tolstoy was deliberately repenting of this early cynicism in making the honourable and conscientious but 'obtuse' young prince the subsequent hero of *Resurrection*. It seems quite likely that he was, for had not he himself renounced the kind of multiple power and perception which he had earlier possessed – powers of perception and analysis that were bound to see through arguments, and remain sceptical about convictions? He was determined now to remain as steadfast in pursuit of his own moral goals and ideals as he represents Nekhlyudov as having become. Nekhlyudov is wholly different from such a hero as Pierre, or even Levin, who are always capable of 'self-derision' and of 'understanding', without committing themselves to a single position. They are seekers, but not dogmatists. At the same time, Tolstoy in fact represents his prince very sympathetically from any angle, together with the repentant and reformed will and ideals which keep him rigidly in his place in the novel. If Nekhlyudov were less sympathetic as a character, *Resurrection* would be more merely a moral parable than it in fact is.

For the old devil, or old genius, of analytic accuracy is still active in Tolstoy, joining hands over the years, as it were, with his younger self. Attempting to live by the will, and 'past the point beyond which one can only see empty phrases', the young prince in the early work befriends a poor student whom he does not in fact like. The student too feels uncomfortable in this relationship, and the narrator, who is described as 'self-satisfied' in his role as 'understander', is amused to see the prince looking cheerful both because he has been kind to the student, and because he has temporarily managed to escape from him. This kind of comic situation could never be allowed in *Resurrection*, and yet it hovers in the background of Maslova's own down-to-earth perception of her lover and benefactor. She is well aware that Nekhlyudov's obstinate attachment is not wholly moral and philanthropic, but that he desires also (as Nekhlyudov's sister long ago said of him, though in a kindly way) to 'appear remarkable in his own eyes'. Gifted at one point, perhaps not wholly convincingly, with Tolstoy's own powers of penetrative perception, Maslova remarks that the prince 'desires to use me spiritually, as he has done physically'.

The nice thing about the prince – and his creator makes us feel this – is that he accepted from her the truth of this with the humility he has genuinely learnt. And yet Tolstoy at once seems to become nervous, lest the reader catch any inkling of scepticism or irreverence. The humour which surrounded Pierre, and even Levin, is now quite banished; and the decisions of the will, once so much humanized and complicated by a sense of the ludicrous, are now uncompromisingly respected. We are reminded continually of the joy and peace which Nekhlyudov feels in having made up his mind once and for all (something Tolstoy himself yearned to do) and nothing can be allowed to disturb this. The reader has the impression of being nervously headed away from any other view of the matter.

No wonder Tolstoy was uneasy and frequently despondent as he composed *Resurrection*, because he was, in a sense, writing like a man with his strongest hand tied behind his back. He had always distrusted the process of what he called *invention*, of finding things out not involuntarily but by conscientious enquiry, and that was the method he had necessarily to use in the composition of *Resurrection*. 'All untrue, invented, weak', he wrote about it at one moment in his diary. 'It is hard to put right a spoiled thing'. And yet put it right he strove to do, and did; and the virtues of the work, many and keenly to be enjoyed and appreciated, are just as visible as its faults. Although he had to invent and to find out, for example, how convicts were dressed and how they behaved, as if he were a journalist; and although there is an obvious contrast here with Chekhov's first-hand account of the penal settlement of Sakhalin, or Dostoevsky's of 'the House of the Dead', he manages none the less to authenticate the account in his own way, from his own recollections and experiences.

And some of these were very moving. More than in any other of his works, perhaps except his story 'Father Sergius', which was being written about the same time, Tolstoy gives us impressions of poor, lost, unregarded people – women especially – whose pathos lies in their total lack of self-sufficiency or self-protectiveness. They are 'the insulted and injured', but seen with a greater degree of starkness and simplicity than in Dostoevsky, and with a complete absence of rhetoric. No doubt Tolstoy sometimes yearned wistfully to be such a person himself. That is certainly the impression the reader gets from the moving story of Father Sergius, where the rock-bottom arrogance and confidence of this ex-Guards officer, even though he has now become a humble priest and anchorite, is contrasted with the 'insignificant and pitiable' woman Pashenka, who has never even been aware of the possibility of standing up for herself. For Father Sergius has become humble by an act of the will, whereas Pashenka is just like that anyway: and remembering 'this thin little girl with large mild eyes and a timid pathetic face', whom he had known as a child, Sergius clutches at the memory as at a last straw. Significantly it is a childhood recollection of family life which the old man, like his creator, clings to in his baffled search for selflessness and sexlessness.

The best thing in *Resurrection*, and the one that most brings back its author's earlier mastery, though in a new and chastened form, is the quick clear sketches of individuals met on the journey (the initial march of the convicts across Moscow is one of the set-pieces of the book). Maslova herself is the prime example: Tolstoy seeming to acknowledge when describing her that there is nothing to describe, or that it lies too deep for him to bring out, or for his Prince Nekhlyudov to understand. Looking at him out of her 'unfathomable squinting eyes' she is as much a stranger to Nekhlyudov at the end of the book as she was when at the beginning, a 16-year-old black-eyed charmer, she played hide-and-seek beside the nettle patch in the garden. Never an 'understander', Nekhlyudov is in any case not concerned to know her (and thus to be able really to love her) because he is too concerned with the duty of making a full atonement to her. Tolstoy cannot, as it were, refrain from this piercing perception, even though he is determinedly loyal throughout to Nekhlyudov's need to make such an atonement, and his honest integrity in attempting to do so.

In one of his early drafts for the novel the pair do eventually marry, and escape from Siberia to England, where Maslova proceeds to help Nekhlyudov, thanks to the new education he has given her, with his work on Henry George, the progressive economist. No doubt it was just as well that Tolstoy decided to scrap this somehow fatally banal consummation. Instead he invented Simonson, the kindly cranky political prisoner whom Maslova falls in love with platonically. And he leaves the story open-minded, with the implication that these various possibilities do not greatly matter. Simonson is cautiously presented as an eccentric but wholly admirable man, and Tolstoy reserves all his old sharpness for his portrait of Novodvorov, the crafty revolutionary, whose self-regard is much greater than his intellect, and who seizes the chance of a 'free union' with any emancipated female revolutionary while privately despising all women as stupid and insignificant.

Over all these late works, except *Hadji Murad,* broods the shadow of Tolstoy's own cranky revulsion from sex (the thing that most aroused the ire and contempt of an otherwise admiring D. H. Lawrence) and his refusal to allow it a position in his own intelligence, or to be looked at except with disgust. The 'Seer of the Flesh', in Merezhkovsky's expressive phrase, has tried to abandon the very force which keeps the flesh alive. Tolstoy in fact comes close at one moment to seeing that his hero pursues his policy of atonement in order to mortify his own flesh rather than to redeem the woman it wronged. The living body has become a corpse, and one of the book's most telling moments is when, at the court-room for Maslova's trial, Nekhlyudov sees the huge corpse of a murdered merchant. 'Maslova's life, the serous liquid oozing from the nostrils of the corpse, the eyes protruding from their sockets, and his own treatment of Maslova, all *seemed to belong to the same order of things'* (my italics). A nasty smell, as Maurice Bering observed, is always apparent in these late tales, however powerful they may be, and Tolstoy seems determined to keep it as nasty in *Resurrection* as it was in *The Kreutzer Sonata*. Rather than the black bag of Ivan Ilyich, it is the spectre of physical decay that haunts him now, transforming the *zhivaya zhizn*, the living life of family and generation, men and women, into what is repulsive and dead.

Tolstoy's flight from his family, and all it had come to stand for, was also an attempt to fly from death. The two had become aspects of the same terrible threat to his being. But in the end it was only death that could save him, at the railway station of Astapovo, from the loving or predatory pursuit of his own family. It was the ideal of the family, the extended Russian family, that had once been at the heart of his work. It had saved Russia, in war and in peace, and insensibly (for Tolstoy's greatest work never seems consciously didactic) it had outflanked and overcome 'systems' of all kinds – the French and Napoleonic system that had so wantonly invaded Russia, the tyrannic system of the state and the tsar. Again and again, in his greatest work, Tolstoy draws this implicit comparison between the systems that both organize and dehumanize human life, and the family and individual instincts that preserve it. In his novel *Dr Zhivago* Pasternak was to draw the same kind of picture, though in far more consciously symbolic tones.

'Consciousness', says Tolstoy at the end of *War and Peace*, 'gives expression to the essence of freedom', while 'reason gives expression to the laws of inevitability'. We are aware of both great forces at work in his creations, and of the relationship between them – 'only by uniting them do we get a clear conception of man's life'. In family life, as in art itself, which in an important sense it resembles, 'freedom is the content and inevitability the form'. In systemic life, whether the system is a communist tyranny or any other, freedom is, as Lenin put it, the recognition of necessity.

There is a subtle and important difference here of which Tolstoy as an artist was fully aware; and the conception of art which he gives us at the end of *War and Peace* is far more profound and more faithful to its author's real achievement than is the official and systemic theory later given in *What is Art?* Tolstoy's world embraces in the fullest sense both that of our solipsistic individual consciousness, and that of a corresponding external inevitability. Many more modern novelists insist on the first and ignore the second. In the world of Tolstoy's great novels we feel that everything happens as it has to happen, but also, where the individual is concerned, as he or she needed it to happen. Freedom and inevitability are in accord: no single view of living preponderates. And this majestic creation of harmony 'calms and satisfies us', in Matthew Arnold's phrase about great art, 'as nothing else can'.

Select Bibliography

WORKS BY TOLSTOY

Primary Source

Polnoe sobranie sochinenii ('Full Collected Works'), 90 vols. (Moscow–Leningrad, 1928–59).

Translated into English

Main editions

Tolstoy Centenary Edition, translated by Louise and Aylmer Maude, 21 vols. Tolstoy Society for Oxford University Press (London: Charles Milford, 1929–37).

Great Short Works of Leo Tolstoy, translated by Louise and Aylmer Maude (New York: Harper and Row, 1967).

The Portable Tolstoy, edited by John Bayley (New York: Penguin, 1978).

Tolstoy's Letters, edited and introduced by R. F. Christian, 2 vols. (London: The Athlone Press, 1978).

Tolstoy's Diaries, edited and translated by R. F. Christian, 2 vols. (London: The Athlone Press, 1985; abridged version, London: Flamingo, 1994).

Tolstoy: Plays, vol. 1, *1856–1886*, translated by Marvin Kantor with Tanya Tulchinsky (Evanston, Ill: Northwestern University Press, 1994).

Available single works and minor collections in paperback (listed in the chronological order in which Tolstoy wrote them)

Childhood, Boyhood, Youth, translated by Rosemary Edmonds (Harmondsworth: Penguin, 1964).

The Raid and Other Stories, translated by Louise and Aylmer Maude, edited by P. N. Furbank (Oxford: Oxford University Press, The World's Classics, 1982).

The Sebastopol Sketches, translated by David McDuff (Harmondsworth: Penguin, 1986).

The Cossacks / Happy Ever After / The Death of Ivan Ilyich, translated by Rosemary Edmonds (Harmondsworth: Penguin, 1960).

War and Peace, translated by Rosemary Edmonds (Harmondsworth: Penguin, 1957).

War and Peace, The Maude Translation: Backgrounds and Sources: Essays in Criticism, edited by George Gibian (New York: Norton, 1966).

War and Peace, translated by Louise and Aylmer Maude, edited by Henry Gifford (Oxford: Oxford University Press, The World's Classics, 1991).

Anna Karenin, translated by Rosemary Edmonds (Harmondsworth: Penguin, 1954).

Anna Karenina, The Maude Translation: Backgrounds and Sources, Essays in Criticism, edited by George Gibian (New York: Norton, 1970).

Anna Karenina, translated by Louise and Aylmer Maude, introduction by John Bayley (Oxford: Oxford University Press, The World's Classics, 1980); new edition with introduction by W. Gareth Jones, 1996.

A Confession and Other Religious Writings, translated by Jane Kentish (Harmondsworth: Penguin, 1987).

Fyodor Dostoyevsky, *Notes from Underground* / Lev Tolstoy, *A Confession*, edited by A. D. P. Briggs (London: Everyman, 1994).

How Much Land Does a Man Need? and other stories, translated by Ronald Wilks (Harmondsworth: Penguin, 1993).

The Kreutzer Sonata and other stories, translated by David McDuff, (Harmondsworth: Penguin, 1985).

Master and Man and other stories, translated by Paul Foote (Harmondsworth: Penguin, 1977).

The Kingdom of God is Within You, translated by Constance Garnett (Lincoln: University of Nebraska Press, 1984).

What is Art?, edited by Gareth Jones, translated by Aylmer Maude (London: Bristol Classical Press, 1994).

Resurrection, translated by Rosemary Edmonds (Harmondsworth: Penguin, 1966).

Resurrection, translated by Louise Maude, edited by Richard. F. Gustafson (Oxford: Oxford University Press, The World's Classics, 1993).

BIOGRAPHICAL AND CRITICAL STUDIES

Adelman, Gary, *Anna Karenina: The Bitterness of Ecstasy* (Boston: Twayne Publishers, 1990).

Armstrong, Judith, *The Unsaid Anna Karenina* (Basingstoke and London: Macmillan, 1988).

Bayley, John, *Tolstoy and the Novel* (London: Chatto and Windus, 1966).

Bloom, Harold (ed.), *Leo Tolstoy* (New York: Chelsea House, 1986).

Bloom, Harold (ed.), *Leo Tolstoy's 'Anna Karenina'* (New York: Chelsea House, 1987).

Bloom, Harold (ed.), *Leo Tolstoy's 'War and Peace'* (New York: Chelsea House, 1988).

Cain, T. G. S., *Tolstoy* (London: Paul Elek, 1977).

Christian, R. F., *Tolstoy's 'War and Peace': A Study* (Oxford: Clarendon Press, 1962).

Christian, R. F., *Tolstoy: A Critical Introduction* (Cambridge: Cambridge University Press, 1969).

Crankshaw, Edward, *Tolstoy: The Making of a Novelist* (New York: Viking, 1974).

Eikhenbaum, Boris, *The Young Tolstoy*, translated by Gary Kern (Ann Arbor: Ardis, 1972).

Eikhenbaum, Boris, *Tolstoi in the Sixties*, translated by Duffield White (Ann Arbor: Ardis, 1982).

Eikhenbaum, Boris, *Tolstoi in the Seventies*, translated by A. Kaspin (Ann Arbor: Ardis, 1982).

Evans, Mary, *Reflecting on Anna Karenina* (London: Routledge, 1989).

Fodor, Alexander, *Tolstoy and the Russians* (Ann Arbor: Ardis, 1984).

Gibian, George, *Tolstoy and Shakespeare* (The Hague: Mouton, 1957).

Gifford, Henry (ed.), *Leo Tolstoy: A Critical Anthology* (Harmondsworth: Penguin, 1971).

Gifford, Henry, *Tolstoy* (Oxford: Oxford University Press, Past Masters, 1982).

Greenwood, E. B., *Tolstoy: The Comprehensive Vision* (London: Methuen, 1980).

Gustafson, Richard F., *Leo Tolstoy, Resident and Stranger* (Princeton: Princeton University Press, 1986).

Hayman, Ronald, *Tolstoy* (London: Routledge and Kegan Paul, 1970).

Jahn, Gary, *The Death of Ivan Ilyich* (New York: Twayne Publishers, 1993).

Jones, Malcolm V. (ed.),. *New Essays on Tolstoy* (Cambridge: Cambridge University Press, 1978).

Knowles, A. V. (ed.), *Tolstoy: The Critical Heritage* (London: Routledge and Kegan Paul, 1978).

Lavrin, Janko, *Tolstoy: An Approach* (London: Methuen, 1944; New York: Russell and Russell, 1968).

Lehrman, Edgar, *A Guide to the Russian Texts of Tolstoy's 'War and Peace'* (Ann Arbor: Ardis, 1979).

McLean, Hugh (ed.), *In the Shade of the Giant* (Berkeley: University of California Press, 1989).

Matlaw, Ralph E. (ed.), *Tolstoy: A Collection of Critical Essays* (Englewood Cliffs, NJ: Prentice-Hall, 1967); includes essays by Merezhkovsky and Shestov.

Maude, Aylmer, *The Life of Tolstoy*, 2 vols. (Oxford: Oxford University Press, 1930, 1987).

Morson, Gary Saul, *Hidden in Plain View: Narrative and Creative Potentials in 'War and Peace'* (Stanford: Stanford University Press, 1987).
Orwin, Donna Tussing, *Tolstoy's Art and Thought, 1847–1880*, (Princeton: Princeton University Press, 1993).
Piraino, Anthony, *A Psychological Study of Tolstoy's 'Anna Karenina'* (San Francisco: EmText, 1993).
Rancour-Laferriere, Daniel, *Tolstoy's Pierre Bezukhov: A Psychoanalytical Study* (London: Bristol Classical Press, 1993).
Redpath, Theodore, *Tolstoy* (London: Bowes and Bowes, 1960).
Rowe, William W., *Leo Tolstoy* (Boston: Twayne Publishers, 1986).
Schultze, Sydney, *The Structure of Anna Karenina* (Ann Arbor: Ardis, 1982).
Shklovsky, Viktor, *Lev Tolstoy*, translated by Olga Shartse (Moscow: Progress, 1978).
Silbajoris, Rimvydas, *Tolstoy's Aesthetics and His Art* (Columbus, Ohio: Slavica, 1991).
Silbajoris, Rimvydas, *War and Peace: Tolstoy's Mirror of the World* (New York: Twayne Publishers, 1995).
Simmons, Ernest J., *Tolstoy* (London: Routledge and Kegan Paul, 1973).
Stenbock-Fermor, E., *The Architecture of 'Anna Karenina': A History of its Writing, Structure, Message* (Lisse: Peter de Ridder Press, 1975).
Thorlby, Anthony, *Leo Tolstoy: Anna Karenina* (Cambridge: Cambridge University Press, Landmarks of World Literature, 1987).
Tolstoy, Sophia, *The Diaries of Sophia Tolstoy*, translated by Cathy Porter (New York: Random House, 1985).
Troyat, Henri, *Tolstoy*, translated by Nancy Amphoux (Harmondsworth: Penguin, 1970).
Turner, C. J. G., *Anna Karenina Companion* (Waterloo, Ont.: Wilfred Laurier University Press, 1994).
Wasiolek, Edward, *Tolstoy's Major Fiction* (Chicago and London: University of Chicago Press, 1978).
Wasiolek, Edward (ed.), *Critical Essays on Tolstoy* (Boston: G. K. Hall, 1986).
Williams, Gareth, *The Influence of Tolstoy on Readers of his Work* (Lewiston, NY and Lampeter: Edwin Mellen Press, 1990).
Williams, Gareth, *Tolstoy's 'Childhood'* (London: Bristol Classical Press, 1995).
Wilson, A. N., *Tolstoy* (London: Hamilton, 1988; Harmondsworth: Penguin, 1989).

GENERAL

Arnold, Matthew, *Essays in Criticism*, 2nd series (London: Macmillan, 1947). Includes his 'Count Leo Tolstoy', which is also to be found in Wasiolek, *Critical Essays on Tolstoy*, above.

Berlin, Isaiah, *Russian Thinkers* (Harmondsworth: Penguin, 1979). Includes his 'The Hedgehog and the Fox', also available as separate volume.

Davie, Donald (ed.), *Russian Literature and Modern English Fiction* (Chicago and London: University of Chicago Press, 1965). Includes D. H. Lawrence, 'Thomas Hardy, Verga and Tolstoy'; and Henry Gifford and Raymond Williams, 'D. H. Lawrence and "Anna Karenina"'.

Freeborn, Richard, *The Rise of the Russian Novel* (Cambridge: Cambridge University Press, 1973).

James, Henry, *The Art of the Novel* (New York: Scribner's, 1962).

Layton, Susan, *Russian Literature and Empire: Conquest of the Caucasus from Pushkin to Tolstoy* (Cambridge: Cambridge University Press, 1994).

Leavis, F. R., *Anna Karenina and Other Essays* (London: Chatto and Windus, 1967).

Mirsky, D. S., *A History of Russian Literature* (New York: Knopf, 1949).

Moser, Charles A. (ed.), *The Cambridge History of Russian Literature* (Cambridge: Cambridge University Press, 1989).

Nabokov, Vladimir, *Lectures on Russian Literature* (London: Picador, 1982).

Orwell, George, 'Lear, Tolstoy and the Fool', in *The Collected Essays, Journalism and Letters of George Orwell*, vol. IV (New York: Harcourt, Brace and World, 1968).

Phelps, Gilbert, *The Russian Novel in English Fiction* (London: Hutchinson, 1956).

Steiner, George, *Tolstoy or Dostoevsky: An Essay in the Old Criticism* (New York: Random House, 1959; Harmondsworth: Penguin, 1967; Chicago: University of Chicago Press, 1985).

Terras, Victor, *A History of Russian Literature* (New Haven and London: Yale University Press, 1991).

Wachtel, Andrew Baruch, *The Battle for Childhood: Creation of a Russian Myth* (Stanford: Stanford University Press, 1990).

Wachtel, Andrew Baruch, *An Obsession with History: Russian Writers Confront the Past* (Stanford: Stanford University Press, 1994).

Ziolkowski, Margaret, *Hagiography and Modern Russian Literature* (Princeton: Princeton University Press, 1988).

Index

WRITERS AND THEIR WORK

"... this series promises to outshine its own obviously high reputation."
Times Higher Education Supplement

"... will build into a fine multi-volume critical encyclopaedia of English literature."
Library Review & Reference Review

"... Excellent, informative, readable, and recommended."
NATE News

"written by outstanding contemporary critics, whose expertise is flavoured by unashamed enthusiasm for their subjects and the series' diverse aspirations."
Times Educational Supplement

"A useful and timely addition to the ranks of the lit crit and reviews genre. Written in an accessible and authoritative style."
Library Association Record

WRITERS AND THEIR WORK

Title	Author
Alfred Tennyson	*Seamus Perry*
Anita Desai	*Elaine Yee Lin Ho*
Anthony Trollope	*Andrew Sanders*
Byron	*Drummond Bone*
C.S. Lewis	*William Gray*
Charles Dickens	*Rod Mengham*
Chinua Achebe	*Nahem Yousaf*
D.H. Lawrence	*Linda Ruth Williams*
E.M. Forster	*Nicholas Royle*
Franz Kafka	*Michael Wood*
George Eliot	*Josephine McDonagh*
George Orwell	*Douglas Kerr*
Gerard Manley Hopkins	*Daniel Brown*
Harold Pinter	*Mark Taylor-Batty*
Henrik Ibsen, 2nd edition	*Sally Ledger*
Henry James—The Later Writing	*Barbara Hardy*
Jane Austen	*Robert Miles*
John Keats	*Kelvin Everest*
Joseph Conrad	*Cedric Watts*
Leo Tolstoy	*John Bayley*
Oscar Wilde	*Alexandra Warwick*
Paul Scott	*Jacqueline Banerjee*
Percy Bysshe Shelley	*Paul Hamilton*
Philip Larkin, 2nd Edition	*Laurence Lerner*
Robert Browning	*John Woolford*
Rudyard Kipling	*Jan Montefiore*
Samuel Beckett	*Sinéad Mooney*

WRITERS AND THEIR WORK

Title	Author
Samuel Taylor Coleridge	*Stephen Bygrave*
Shashi Deshpande	*Amrita Bhalla*
Sir Walter Scott	*Harriet Harvey Wood*
Stephen Crane	*Kevin J. Hayes*
Swinburne	*Catherine Maxwell*
Sylvia Plath, 2nd edition	*Elisabeth Bronfen*
T.S. Eliot	*Colin MacCabe*
Ted Hughes	*Susan Bassnett*
Thomas Hardy, 2nd Edition	*Peter Widdowson*
V.S. Naipaul	*Suman Gupta*
Victorian Quest Romance	*Robert Fraser*
Virginia Woolf, 2nd Edition	*Laura Marcus*
W.B. Yeasts	*Edward Larrissy*
William Blake	*Steve Vine*
William Golding, 2nd Edition	*Kevin McCarron*
William Makepeace Thackeray	*Richard Salmon*
Wole Soyinka	*Mpalive-Hangson Msiska*